BARRY KNIGHT

RETHINKING POVERTY

What makes a good society?

POLICY PRESS SHORTS INSIGHTS

First published in Great Britain in 2017 by

Policy Press
University of Bristol
1-9 Old Park Hill
Bristol
BS2 8BB
UK
t: +44 (0)117 954 5940
pp-info@bristol.ac.uk
www.policypress.co.uk

North America office:
Policy Press
c/o The University of Chicago Press
1427 East 60th Street
Chicago, IL 60637, USA
t: +1 773 702 7700
f: +1 773 702 9756
sales@press.uchicago.edu
www.press.uchicago.edu

British Library Cataloguing in Publication Data
A catalogue record for this book is available from the British Library.

Library of Congress Cataloging-in-Publication Data
A catalog record for this book has been requested.

ISBN 978-1-4473-4060-7 (paperback)
ISBN 978-1-4473-4061-4 (ePub)
ISBN 978-1-4473-4062-1 (Mobi)
ISBN 978-1-4473-4063-8 (ePDF)

Cover design by Policy Press
Front cover: image kindly supplied by Getty
Printed and bound in Great Britain by CMP, Poole
Policy Press uses environmentally responsible print partners

Contents

List of figures and tables

Figures

Tables

Acknowledgements

A great many people and organisations have contributed to this book. Most are acknowledged in the text, but three people deserve special recognition and thanks. Andrew Milner provided first class research assistance, Caroline Hartnell gave outstanding editorial support and Georgia Smith organised excellent communications.

Webb Memorial Trustees provided support and supervision while giving me freedom to develop the research and interpret results. All views expressed here are mine and do not necessarily represent those of the Trust.

Barry Knight

Foreword

This book explores what a good society without poverty could look like and identifies policies and practices to support it. There is now widespread acceptance that neoliberalism has gone too far, while the welfare state established after the Second World War is in decline. Yet no alternative approaches have so far emerged. This book helps to fill that gap.

It is based on a five-year programme of research supported by the Webb Memorial Trust. Research partners include leading organisations such as Compass, the Child Poverty Action Group (CPAG), the Centre for Local Economic Strategies, the Town and Country Planning Association (TCPA), the Fabian Society, Bright Blue, Oxfam, the Smith Institute, Shelter and others, as well as a range of academics. We have also worked closely with the All Party Parliamentary Group on Poverty. Barry Knight led this work. In this book he brings together the findings of the various strands of the research and suggests ways to take it forward.

This book has its origins in the work of a pioneering social reformer whose lifetime of research enabled much of the social advance of the 20th century but who is now largely forgotten: Beatrice Webb (1858–1943). Her *Minority Report of the Royal Commission on the Poor Laws and Relief of Distress 1905–09* was about more than just breaking up the Poor Law. It raised new ideas, which she developed with her husband Sidney, such as organising the labour market to prevent unemployment, providing a national health service and operating universal social services. Working closely with their friend William Beveridge, they were highly influential with academics and senior politicians and laid the intellectual foundations for what became the welfare state.

To commemorate the centenary of the Minority Report, the Trust commissioned the Fabian Society to produce *The solidarity society: Fighting poverty and inequality in an age of affluence 1909–2009.*[1] The book addressed the problem of poverty, which had persisted despite the progress of the previous 100 years. However, many proposals entailed increased state spending and, following the financial crash of 2008 and the austerity policies emerging from the 2010 Coalition government, it was unlikely that the book's proposals would be taken up.

The Trust therefore commissioned two pieces of research: a review of social policy since 1945, undertaken by the Smith Institute, to identify which policies were effective in reducing poverty,[2] and a series of essays from academics and practitioners in which they were asked to imagine what Beatrice Webb would suggest doing about poverty now.[3] Following these publications, the Trust concluded that traditional social policy is inadequate to deal with the challenges facing the UK and produced a consultation document: *Beatrice Webb: A fitting legacy*. Its publication in 2012 set out the prospectus for the research described here.

The book reframes the debate about poverty and how a good society should eliminate it. We hope that this research, like that of the Webbs, will stimulate our partners and others to develop their ideas and help to create the society we want, rather than the society we have.

Richard Rawes
Chair, Webb Memorial Trust

Notes

[1] Horton, T. and Gregory, J. (2009) *The solidarity society: Fighting poverty in an age of affluence 1909–2009*, London: Fabian Society and Webb Memorial Trust.

[2] Coates, D. (2012) *From the Poor Law to Welfare to Work: What have we learned from a century of anti-poverty policies?*, London: Smith Institute and the Webb Memorial Trust.

[3] Knight, B. (ed) (2011) *A minority view: What Beatrice Webb would say now*, London: Alliance Publishing Trust and Webb Memorial Trust.

Introduction

In 1909, at the launch of her *Minority Report of the Royal Commission on the Poor Laws and Relief of Distress 1905–09*, Beatrice Webb said: 'It is now possible to abolish destitution.'[1]

In the intervening years, we have almost succeeded, though destitution's close family relative – poverty – is still with us. Poverty spoils lives, costs public money and destabilises social relations in a cycle that passes from one generation to the next. We may have done away with the humiliation of the 19th-century soup kitchen, but we are fast replacing it with the humiliation of the 21st-century foodbank.[2] Given the scale of our social, economic and technological advance, it is remarkable that we allow this continuing stain on our society.

The persistence of poverty was the starting point for the Webb Memorial Trust's research. In surveying the field, the Trust found an abundance of research describing the problem of poverty, but little on solutions.[3] Moreover, available remedies tended to rely on discrete technocratic policy fixes to address symptoms, rather than focusing on the complex societal processes that produce poverty in the first place.

The Trust's research addresses those complex societal processes and, in so doing, suggests that success depends on reframing the approach. Rather than addressing what we don't want – poverty – the research looks at what we do want: a society without poverty. Such positive framing helps to transcend the problem of poverty and address it at a higher level. The task of this book is, therefore, not to repair an old system that appears incapable of eradicating poverty, but instead to support a process of redesigning a society in which poverty becomes obsolete. This entails dealing with normative as well as theoretical, empirical and practical matters.

The study had three main framing questions:

- What is a good society without poverty?
- How do we obtain that society?
- Who does what to implement a good society without poverty?

The research looks at these questions from many different angles. Studies include the perspectives of people living in poverty, the participation of community activists, children's voices, and population surveys of more than 12,000 people. Topics covered include economic development, employment, social security, housing, planning, civil society and community development. A wide range of research partners were involved.

Answers to the framing questions suggest that the two narratives that have dominated Britain since the Second World War no longer have resonance among the mass of the population. First, society can no longer rely on the 'social administration' approach, in which state policies are designed from the top down to meet social needs. Pioneered by Beatrice Webb, adapted by William Beveridge, developed further by Richard Titmuss and brought to fruition by Peter Townsend, the social administration approach worked reasonably well for the three decades following the Second World War, but has now lost its purchase. Second, the neoliberal narrative, pioneered by Frederick von Hayek and Milton Friedman and based on the idea of economic growth, a free market, low tax, individual liberty, rewards for entrepreneurs and ever-decreasing public investment no longer works either.

The new narrative developed here is dominated by social factors rather than economic ones. While being bold in asserting this, the Trust is aware of what Tony Crosland called 'the vulgar fallacy that some ideal society can be said to exist, of which blueprints can be drawn, and which will be ushered in as soon as certain specific reforms have been delivered'.[4]

No research report can deliver answers from on high and expect them to be applied directly. Recent events, most notably the wholesale rejection of the views of the establishment in the referendum on Britain's future in the European Union, make it clear that such an approach has lost whatever currency it may once have had.

Rather than offering any sort of blueprint, the Trust's approach is to produce ideas based on robust research that other people, policy makers and agencies can make use of in striving to develop the society we want. Perspectives come from different parts of the political spectrum and have been disseminated through the All Party Parliamentary Group on Poverty. This aligns with a key finding in the research that, if we are to make progress towards a good society, there is no monopoly of view that can or should hold sway.

Positive developments will occur when people move beyond their fixed opinions and narrow organisational interests to think about an inclusive process of development. The narrative set out here is meant to be the first draft of a guide for such a process. The text should be developed organically so that it has wide ownership based on the principles lying behind what people want their society to be.

In compiling this volume, the Trust is aware that the report is not comprehensive. While in all the areas described here there is more data than can be reported in the space available, some important areas – education and health, for example – have not been addressed at all. The main goal is not comprehensiveness, but to promote a new way of framing how we see poverty and to report material that might be helpful in enabling us to move society forward.

A central tenet of the approach, emphasised throughout the book, is that we cannot lay down hard-and-fast rules to prescribe what a good society would look like or how we can achieve it. Such top-down technocratic fixes have been shown not to work. The book sets out five principles for a good society without poverty, based on the research.

But the five principles are merely a starting point; they are to be developed, modified and applied by people and organisations who want to take the ideas forward. In constructing a good society, process is as important as product. If we are to produce the society we want, we need to engage people over time and use creative methods to develop ideas and approaches. The book is intended as a step along the way.

Notes

[1]   Coates, D. (2012) *From the Poor Law to Welfare to Work: What have we learned from a century of anti-poverty policies?*, London: Smith Institute and the Webb Memorial Trust, p 4.
[2]   Garthwaite, K. (2016) *Hunger pains: Life inside foodbank Britain*, Bristol: Policy Press.
[3]   Knight, B. (ed) (2011) *A minority view: What Beatrice Webb would say now*, London: Alliance Publishing Trust and Webb Memorial Trust
[4]   Crosland, C.A.R. (1956) *The Future of socialism*, London: Jonathan Cape, 216.

ONE

The narrative on poverty has failed

This chapter examines our understanding of poverty and reviews its history since Beatrice Webb's 1909 Minority Report.[1] It reaches three main conclusions. First, the language that informed the development of the welfare state has lost its power. Second, the way that organisations working to reduce poverty describe their work may be doing more harm than good. Third, we need to reframe the way we think about poverty.

Language matters

Organisations working to end poverty have come to recognise that the narrative which has informed approaches to poverty since the 1942 Beveridge Report no longer works. So-called 'expert' opinion about poverty is out of step with how most people view it.

In January 2016, the Webb Memorial Trust, together with Shelter and Oxfam, convened 25 leading charities to discuss the language of poverty. A consistent refrain was that campaigns to reduce poverty are increasingly falling on deaf ears.[2] Structural explanations of poverty have little resonance because people blame the poor themselves for their plight. Fact-based campaigns to explode the 'myths of poverty' reinforce, rather than challenge, stereotypes of people on benefits. The result is that the public argument is being lost. Writing in the *New Statesman* in October 2016, Justin Watson from Oxfam admitted that charities are getting it wrong:

> There is a growing consensus that the narratives used by the third sector, however well-meaning and 'right', have been rejected. Take 'poverty', a term that is politically divisive, laced with stigma and highly contested, to the point of still having to persuade people that it exists at all in the UK.[3]

A common strategy for charities and poverty campaigners is to express outrage at injustice. Such a tactic yields little result. For example, in a Trust-supported study, Olivia Bailey, research director at the Fabian Society, found that inequality is a 'defining feature of our age', but 'talking about inequality describes a problem, it doesn't generate enthusiasm for a solution'.[4] An earlier Trust publication, *The society we want*, discussed how a constant stream of publications on poverty from respected academics and think tanks did little to solve the problem.[5] It showed that constant repetition of a problem makes matters worse because people come to believe that the problem is so great that they can play no part in finding a solution.

The Trust brought together 35 community activists from all over the UK for a meeting at the Wilberforce Centre of Slavery and Emancipation in Hull to think about solutions. Their conclusion was:

> Tear up the old script. It's false and harmful. The media uses it to bully the poor and vulnerable, showing them as objects of ridicule or revulsion. The government, meanwhile, seems not just indifferent, but hostile. The solidarity which once bound people to each other has been eroded leaving poor people isolated and anxious. If we are going to change this, we need different ways of communicating. We are too prone to talk just to ourselves. If we carry on doing that, how on earth will we convince others?[6]

This sentiment has been repeated many times during the research. A new framing is necessary to enable all those working to end poverty to speak with one voice, to collaborate rather than to compete, and to enable those directly affected to speak rather than be spoken for.

The Joseph Rowntree Foundation has taken up this challenge by undertaking research with the National Children's Bureau and FrameWorks Institute, a US-based non-profit that develops effective public discourse about social issues. The goal is to develop a new way of communicating about poverty in the UK based on how the public thinks about poverty, not just what they say. This approach maps the 'expert story' onto public understanding, partly by identifying the gaps between the two. The outcome will be a set of communications tools that expand public understanding of poverty.[7]

Poverty is ambiguous

A key challenge is the word 'poverty' itself. Despite a voluminous literature on poverty stretching over many centuries, there is little agreement about definition, measurement, causes and solutions.

Let us start with definition. The *Merriam-Webster Dictionary* defines poverty as 'the state of one who lacks a usual or socially acceptable amount of money or material possessions'. It lists synonyms, including: penury, destitution, indigence, pennilessness, privation, deprivation, impoverishment, neediness, need, want, hardship, impecuniousness, impecuniosity, hand-to-mouth existence, beggary, pauperism, straitened circumstances, meagreness, bankruptcy and insolvency.

Absolute poverty and relative poverty

However, the dictionary also points out that poverty 'may cover a range from extreme want of necessities to an absence of material comforts'. This gives an elasticity to the term that not only reduces its usefulness, but also requires that we distinguish between 'absolute poverty' and 'relative poverty'. Absolute poverty means 'lack of sufficient resources with which to meet basic needs'. Relative poverty means 'low income or resources in relation to the average'. These are very different ideas.

A hundred years ago, the priority for action was absolute poverty. In their introduction to *The prevention of destitution*, Sidney and Beatrice Webb noted:

> We are driven to use the word 'destitution' for lack of any better equivalent. We may quote Professor Huxley upon its meaning: 'It is a condition in which food, warmth and clothing, which are necessary for the mere maintenance of the functions of the body in their normal state, cannot be obtained; in which men, women and children are forced to crowd into dens where decency is abolished, and the most ordinary conditions of healthful existence are impossible of attainment; in which the pleasures within reach are reduced to brutality and drunkenness; in which the pains accumulate at compound interest in the shape of starvation, disease, stunted development and moral degradation; in which the prospect of even steady and honest industry is a life of unsuccessful battling with hunger, rounded by a pauper's grave'.[8]

The Webbs' research showed that, judging by successful applications for parochial relief, more than two million people were destitute in 1911. Given that destitution was concentrated in certain areas, such that there were 'cities of the poor', the destitution rate signified 'a disease at the heart of society'.

Today, while we have not totally abolished destitution among certain groups – most evidently among homeless people, migrant workers and refugees – no campaigner would seriously claim that significant sections of the UK's population experience the level of destitution described by the Webbs. Indeed, a 2009 report by the Joseph Rowntree Foundation notes: 'When we talk about poverty in the UK today we rarely mean malnutrition or the levels of squalor of previous centuries or even the hardships of the 1930s before the advent of the welfare state.'[9]

Most expert opinion is now driven by the idea of relative poverty. This occurs when people's standard of living is much lower than the general standard in the country or region in which they live so that they struggle to live a normal life and to participate in ordinary economic, social and cultural activities. While the concept of relative poverty was understood by the Webbs, the first serious study was undertaken by W.G. Runciman in 1966.[10] Peter Townsend developed the idea by using 60 indicators of the population's 'style of living' for a 1968–69 survey of living standards in the UK. According to Townsend:

> Individuals, families and groups in the population can be said to be in poverty when they lack the resources to obtain the types of diet, participate in the activities and have the living conditions and amenities which are customary, or are at least widely encouraged or approved, in the societies to which they belong.[11]

This definition forms the basis of much poverty research today. Joanna Mack and Stewart Lansley used it to pioneer the 'consensual' approach to measuring poverty by investigating, for the first time ever, the public's perceptions of minimum needs. Carried out in 1983 by MORI, their research formed the basis of the ITV series *Breadline Britain*, transmitted in August 1983.[12] At that time, they talked of 'a new type of poverty: resources so low as to exclude people from ordinary living patterns and activities, incomes insufficient to provide a living standard considered normal and essential by the great majority of the population'. The poor were better off than the poor of the past, but still badly off in comparison with the rest of society. Mack and Lansley have continued their work through various surveys right up to this day.

The two concepts of poverty – absolute and relative – give rise to a major communications problem. As part of the Trust's work, it commissioned extensive population studies with YouGov which show two very different understandings of the term. The population is divided between those who think that only absolute poverty matters and those who think that relative poverty is important too.

In 2015, 10,112 people from England, Scotland and Wales were asked: 'Thinking about the government helping those who are not in work, what would be the best form of financial help that the government can provide?' Various options designed to elicit attitudes to absolute and relative poverty were given. Results are shown in Figure 1.1.

The chart shows the division. The largest single response is about absolute poverty and the second largest (with almost the same proportion) is about relative poverty. As will be shown later, the survey data reveals a fault line in attitudes towards poverty. To use the single term 'poverty' to cover these very different situations is likely to lead to ambiguous messages.

Greater clarity could perhaps be found if there was agreement about measurement, but again there is none. A requirement for any measure is that it has high 'face validity' in the sense that people recognise the idea when they see it. With poverty, it is clear from the Trust's and other research that people who are regarded as poor by experts don't necessarily recognise themselves as poor.[13] This means that, as a way of mobilising opinion, poverty fails an important test.

The academic literature includes a variety of measures of poverty. For example, the World Bank defines absolute poverty as a person living on $1.25 per day and moderate poverty as a person living on $2.00 per day. European Union and The Organisation for Economic Co-operation and Development (OECD) definitions tend to be based on relative poverty so that people are classed as poor if their income is up to 60 per cent of the median household income. Recent Joseph Rowntree Foundation work has used a measure based on 75 per cent of the 'Minimum Income Standard', which is a definition of minimum needs based on what members of the public think is essential for a minimum standard of living.

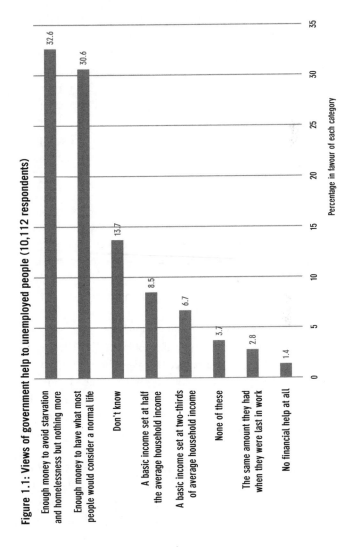

Figure 1.1: Views of government help to unemployed people (10,112 respondents)

Source: YouGov Survey of 10,112 adults from England, Scotland and Wales in January 2015.

Measures other than income

Others suggest that income alone is not a sufficient measure, because it is important to reflect poverty as a multidimensional experience. Describing the approach taken by the Centre for Social Justice, Samantha Callan argues that the 'obsession with income and how much "stuff" people have (the material deprivation measure) ignored the drivers of poverty: entrenched worklessness, family breakdown, problem debt, substandard education and drug and alcohol dependency'.[14] This perspective led to the Coalition government's consultation on broadening the measures of poverty 'because of the need to reflect its multidimensional nature'.

A different approach is evident in the concept of 'social exclusion'. Based on a review of the literature in 2007, Levitas and colleagues define social exclusion as:

> a complex and multi-dimensional process. It involves the lack or denial of resources, rights, goods and services, and the inability to participate in the normal relationships and activities, available to the majority of people in a society, whether in economic, social, cultural or political arenas. It affects both the quality of life of individuals and the equity and cohesion of society as a whole.[15]

A third way of thinking is the 'capabilities approach' associated with Amartya Sen. This stresses the importance of everyone's freedom to achieve the kinds of lives that they value.[16]

The last three approaches to poverty, which take account of multidimensional features, require measurement through the development of an index. Again, there are several such indexes, including the Index of Multiple Deprivation and the Human Development Index.

This brief review shows that poverty is a contested term. According to David Gordon: 'It often seems that if you put five academics (or policy makers) in a room you would get at least six different definitions of poverty.'[17] Although Gordon points out that many of the differences are due to a misunderstanding of the difference between definition and measurement, focus groups run as part of the Trust's research found that the public is confused by the term 'poverty', as illustrated by these two quotations from the focus groups:

'Poverty to me is people starving and children having bare feet. I never see this here personally.'

'I can't afford Sky sports and I am a 68-year-old invalid ... am I in poverty?'

Poverty is toxic

So, not only is the word 'poverty' ambiguous, it is toxic too. In focus groups, use of the term raises the emotional temperature, commonly leading to what Julia Unwin, a former director of the Joseph Rowntree Foundation, called an 'angry and fruitless debate'.[18]

One symptom of the troubled language of poverty is the high prevalence of popular falsehoods. Early in the research, the Trust placed faith in the idea of 'busting the myths of poverty'. To this end, it commissioned Rob MacDonald and Tracy Shildrick to conduct a rigorous academic study of six commonly used statements about poverty:

- There is no real poverty in the UK.
- People on benefits aren't really poor.
- Welfare benefits are too high and create welfare dependency.
- People in poverty are there because of their own failures and behaviour.
- The poor are always with us and nothing can be done.
- Employment is the best route out of poverty.[19]

When examined against the literature on poverty, MacDonald and Shildrick found that none of these statements stand up to empirical scrutiny and they could therefore be classed as popular falsehoods or 'myths'.

To test the value of the myth-busting approach, the Trust commissioned a study of 2,000 individuals from YouGov. The study found three distinct attitudes towards poverty:

- Since poverty is beyond the control of the individual, it is the responsibility of the state, the labour market or some other external agency.
- Since poverty is within the control of the individual, a new set of attitudes and behaviours on the part of the poor is required.
- Since poverty is an inevitable part of society such that 'the poor are always with us', there is nothing to be done about it.

To delve deeper, 12 focus groups were selected from the sample using two different criteria: their attitudes towards poverty (one of the three above) and their income level (high pay, low pay or benefit recipient). The discussion explored many aspects of poverty.

One exercise was to present statistics describing different facts about poverty, for example:

- Some 3.6 million children currently grow up below the poverty line, a figure that is expected to rise to 4.2 million by the year 2020.
- On average people think that 41 per cent of the entire welfare budget goes on benefits to unemployed people, while the true figure is 3 per cent.

Across all focus groups, the findings were consistent. Facts fail to change people's opinions. When presented with a fact that conflicts with their prior opinion, people tend to dismiss it as 'what the government would say' or 'newspaper talk'. This phenomenon is known as 'confirmation bias', in which new information is moulded to fit existing assumptions. "Are these figures compiled by the same people who don't know any true immigration figures?", asked one focus group participant. "I knew the stat about the welfare budget already. I quote it to people", said another. Discussion in the focus groups was highly emotive and dominated by blaming the government or blaming people in poverty depending on participants' attitudes. Feelings, not facts, hold sway in thinking about poverty.

These findings accord with other research, notably by Drew Westen in *The political brain*, showing that facts and rationality play little part when it comes to people's judgements about social issues.[20] And yet the poverty industry in the UK is engaged in a persistent cycle of drawing attention to the bad news about poverty and expecting people to be affected by it. It appears that attempts to counter the dominant narrative with facts that show it is false are pointless, particularly when the facts are drawn from a narrative that has lost its ground. As David Marquand has pointed out, 'The narratives that structured the early post-war period have lost their purchase, but no new narratives have filled the resulting vacuum.'[21]

Poverty campaigners are, however, still apt to use the narrative of the immediate postwar world. Some of the Trust's early commissions fell into the same trap. While the analysis behind the Fabian Society report commissioned to celebrate the centenary of the 1909 Minority Report had merit, its recommendations to increase welfare spending were out of step with the age.[22] Similarly, a report by the Smith Institute in 2012 suggested a return to the principles behind the Beveridge Report.[23] Both reports suggested a strong emphasis on the state as a key agent and saw a return to a contributory principle of welfare with a means test for those who could not meet the contribution requirements. However, the work of John Hudson and Neil Lunt from York University shows declining support for welfare spending since the 1960s, with attitudes changing most dramatically in the past 30 years. In 1987, 60 per cent of people supported the view that there should be increased welfare spending funded by higher taxes, but this figure had fallen to 35 per cent by 2013.[24]

Poverty campaigners are failing. The work on communication by FrameWorks notes:

Communicators face serious challenges in cultivating broad public support for the policies and programmes needed to solve the problem of poverty in the United Kingdom. Many of the public's cultural models of poverty, economic wellbeing and the economy do not support meaningful change.[25]

We need to start from a different place. First, we need to look back to work out how we got here and to assess where we stand now.

The rise and fall of the social administration society

The past 100 years have seen the rise and fall of state intervention as a means of delivering a good society. At the beginning of the 20th century, a new public mood led to efforts to eradicate widespread destitution, sweeping away the Poor Law, and by mid-century developing a welfare state. A different mood characterised the last 30 years of the century as private capital took over as the dominant force in society and relegated public concern about poverty to a minority view.

A landmark report

The first decade of the 20th century saw the first stirrings of public action, first to complement and then to replace private philanthropy as the chief motor for social progress. A landmark report was the *Minority Report of the Royal Commission on the Poor Laws and Relief of Distress 1905–09.*[26] A central tenet of this report was:

Poverty is not a weakness of individual character but a problem of social structure and economic mismanagement.

The report laid the responsibility for solving destitution at the door of government. At the time, the report failed to gain traction. However, 100 years later, at a conference held at the London School of Economics to celebrate it, one participant described the report as 'the most successful failure ever'. The Minority Report eventually led to the abolition of the Poor Law and provided the intellectual principles behind the welfare state. Beveridge noted: 'The Beveridge Report of 1942 stemmed from what all of us had imbibed from the Webbs.'[27] Clement Attlee, the prime minister whose 1945 government implemented the Beveridge Report, was the Webbs' campaign manager for the 1909 Minority Report. He described it as 'the seed from which later blossomed the welfare state'.[28]

Social advance in postwar Britain

The work of Keynes and Beveridge became the basis of the postwar consensus across political parties about how to develop a good society based on the twin pillars of full employment and social security. The key was a mixed economy in which planning played a central role. For the next 30 years, the state took prime responsibility for poverty by committing itself to full employment as a goal of economic policy and to a secure population as a goal of social policy. Free education, healthcare and other social services gave opportunities for all regardless of whether they had the money to pay or not. To avoid the stigma of 'charity', the system was to be paid for by National Insurance, a contributory scheme deducted from people's pay packets.

These developments led to much social advance in the postwar period. In the 1950s, it seemed that the combination of full employment and state welfare would banish poverty forever. Seebohm Rowntree's last study of York in 1951 suggested that poverty had all but disappeared.[29] It seemed that the pain and bitterness of the 1930s depression would fade like a bad dream. Anthony Crosland's *The future of socialism*, published in 1956, suggested that the dark side of capitalism had been tamed, so that top-down planning by the state could be relaxed.[30] In 1957 the Conservative prime minister Harold MacMillan gave a speech in which he said:

'You will see a state of prosperity such as we have never had in my lifetime – nor indeed in the history of this country. Indeed let us be frank about it. Most of our people have never had it so good.'[31]

This social advance was based on four main factors.[32] First, expansionary macroeconomic policies, combined with a commitment to full employment, meant that work was plentiful. Second, strong trade unions in a relatively protected economy meant that real wages rose in tandem with productivity, allowing workers to enjoy rising living standards. Third, public spending on health, education and housing created a social wage that particularly helped those on lower incomes. Fourth, fiscal policy taxed the rich to benefit everyone, including the poor. These four factors combined to create social mobility. People could see that they were better off than their parents and had higher aspirations for their children. The result was what economist Paul Krugman has called the 'great compression'. The incomes of the top and bottom tier of earners converged and poverty was much reduced.[33]

The system unravels

Despite these successes, cracks began to appear in the welfare state. Three main problems emerged which meant that the system began to unravel. First, it was not as effective as people had hoped. As early as 1951 Richard Titmuss was disappointed that the arrangements did nothing to address structural inequality.[34] This conclusion was reinforced in 1972 by James Kincaid, who conducted a comprehensive review of the social security system and concluded that it 'does nothing effective to iron out inequality, and that the services are far less egalitarian and more punitive than is generally supposed'.[35]

Nor did it fully solve poverty. In 1965 Brian Abel-Smith and Peter Townsend 'rediscovered' poverty, finding that Rowntree's 1951 work, which suggested that poverty had disappeared, had studied untypical conditions and reached the wrong conclusions.[36]

Second, there were financial pressures. The National Insurance system could not sustain itself through economic and demographic changes with the effect that the proportion of means-tested benefits increased. National Insurance had been predicated on full employment, male breadwinners, marriage for life and short lives. Rising unemployment meant that the link between work and benefits could not be sustained. Social security spending increased from 4 per cent of GDP in 1948–49 to 11.5 per cent in 1983–84.[37] The 1986 Social Security Act effectively ended the National Insurance principle.

Third, and perhaps most serious of all, the way that it was administered was unpopular with claimants. They resented the 'cold bureaucracies' running the system, and were angry about the size, inflexibility, inaccessibility and impersonality of the apparatus. This led to the formation of 'claimants' unions' in the 1960s. They saw the Department of Health and Social Security as an 'agent of social control' operating with a culture that paid little heed to parliamentary accountability. They campaigned on a four-point platform demanding adequate income without means tests, transparency, no distinction between the deserving and undeserving poor, and a system controlled by those who use it.

End of the consensus

This lack of pride in the system was exploited by those who had never believed in the welfare state. From the outset, a small group plotted its downfall. In 1947 Professor Friedrich von Hayek invited 36 influential people to Switzerland to form the Mont Pelerin Society. The group was diverse, but they had a common bond: 'They see danger in the expansion of government, not least in state welfare, in the power of trade unions and business monopoly, and in the continuing threat and reality of inflation.'[38] The group worked tirelessly 'to facilitate an exchange of ideas between like-minded scholars in the hope of strengthening the principles and practice of a free society and to study the workings, virtues, and defects of market-oriented economic systems'.

In *Thinking the unthinkable* Richard Cockett tells the story of how the ideas of free market economics gained ground through the efforts of organisations such as the Institute of Economic Affairs, the Centre for Policy Studies and the Adam Smith Institute.[39] This was a global movement. In the US, a country that never bought into the idea of the welfare state, conservative think tanks, funded by 12 private foundations, embarked on a long-term and concerted campaign to change policy across the world in favour of tax cuts, privatisation of government services, and deregulation of industry and the environment, as well as deep cuts in government spending. They were well organised, using everything from sound bites to scholarly journals.[40] A key text was Charles Murray's *Losing ground*.[41]

This approach found favour with people who had become increasingly unwilling to pay taxes to support social security for those they regarded as 'scroungers'.[42] This 'tax–welfare' backlash was fuelled by articles in the popular press, some parts of which developed an obsession with 'cheats'.[43]

'Butskellism', the consensus between Labour and Conservatives, ended during the 1970s, when the oil crisis caused by the Arab–Israeli War of 1973 produced stagflation. Keynesian economics buckled under the weight of inflation, unemployment and industrial disorder. From the chaos, a strong leader emerged. Following her election victory in 1979, Margaret Thatcher was determined to reverse Britain's economic decline. She believed that the welfare state, with its cradle-to-grave security, had turned once industrious Britain into a 'dependency culture'. She wanted to replace this with an 'enterprise culture' to raise the status of business, growth, moneymaking and profit. A succession of Conservative governments attempted to free the economy, encouraging individual enterprise, fostering a consumer boom, and seeing the welfare state as a security net of last resort. Reviewing this period of history for the Trust, the Smith Institute concluded:

> According to the Conservative Party, incomes policy had obviously failed, trade unions were too powerful, markets were over-regulated; taxes were too high, nationalised industries were feather bedded and an over generous social welfare system discouraged enterprise and created state dependency.[44]

From the mid-1970s onwards the four factors that produced social mobility went into reverse. The Labour government had already set the scene for the changed direction in public policy. In 1976 the government sought a loan from the International Monetary Fund (IMF) to cope with deteriorating economic conditions, and the IMF demanded large cuts in public spending. The Conservative government of 1979 continued the policy. In subsequent years, unemployment became a normal feature of British society, the universal principles behind the welfare state were eroded, high pay for top executives became the norm, and tax rates for the rich were substantially reduced. This led to the 'great divergence',[45] with an ever-widening gap between rich and poor.

A key turning point was the 1981 recession. The government abandoned its commitment to full employment as a goal of economic policy. Once this had happened, it was a short step to breaking the link between work and benefits, effectively ending the National Insurance principle. People who were out of work were encouraged to go on incapacity benefit rather than unemployment benefit, partly to give the appearance of lower unemployment. For retired people, a big shift occurred in 1981, when state pension increases were tied to prices rather than wages – though it was invariably the latter that rose faster. Means testing became the dominant principle and was enshrined in the 1986 Social Security Act.

Just as government was reducing benefits to individuals, there were the stirrings of the 'me society' as the accumulation of personal wealth became a state-endorsed value. The new mood was exemplified in 1986 when 'Big Bang' – the government's deregulation of the finance industry – freed the City of London to pursue great wealth for the few. This wealth was meant to 'trickle down' to the poor, but it didn't, so poverty increased throughout the 1980s and early 1990s. Child poverty, as measured by household incomes below 60 per cent of the median, doubled between 1979 and 1997.[46]

A new beginning

The incoming Labour government of 1997 took poverty more seriously than any government since the 1960s, even though the word 'poverty' hardly figured in its election manifesto.[47] A decisive announcement was made in 1999 when prime minister Tony Blair made a historic claim: 'Ours is the first generation to end child poverty forever, and it will take a generation. It is a 20-year mission, but I believe it can be done.'[48]

A key instrument in the pursuit of this aim was the Social Exclusion Unit, which was part of the Cabinet Office. Programmes included the National Strategy for Neighbourhood Renewal, a 20-year plan to ensure that no one was disadvantaged because of where they lived. Sure Start was designed to enable children, particularly those from disadvantaged areas, to have the best start in life. There were 'New Deal' programmes to enable those disadvantaged in the labour market to get into work. A national minimum wage was introduced to address in-work poverty, and working tax credits were meant to ensure that people in low-paid work would have higher post-tax incomes than if they were on benefits.

These programmes were partly successful in reducing poverty. Jane Waldfogel evaluated the Labour government's anti-poverty strategy using three main dimensions: promoting work and making work pay; increasing financial support for families with children; and investing in the health, early-life development and education of children.[49] Although outcomes fell short of plans, the strategy nevertheless significantly increased single-parent employment, raised incomes for low-income families, and improved child outcomes. Pensioner poverty fell by one-third between 1998–89 and 2007–08. Poverty fell in the UK while it stagnated elsewhere in the world. The Institute of Fiscal Studies also reviewed Labour's record and concurred that progress had been made, though the gains were largely based on very large increases in benefits and tax increases.[50]

Part of the fragility of the Labour government's approach stemmed from its tendency to pursue social policy by stealth because of its fears of antagonising an electorate increasingly hostile to welfare claimants. As Kate Bell and Jason Streilitz found in a Trust-sponsored review: 'Ending child poverty never really took on political salience outside a narrow policy elite.'[51]

However, Labour managed to obtain cross-party support for the Child Poverty Act 2010, which enshrined in law Tony Blair's 2001 pledge to end child poverty by 2020.

The crash and its aftermath

The financial crisis of 2008 produced an economic shock that ushered in austerity policies. The Coalition government came to power in the middle of a period of large falls in workers' pay. Between 2009 and 2011 – a period that neatly sandwiched the May 2010 election – median weekly earnings fell by 7 per cent in real terms.

Robert Joyce and Luke Sibieta from the Institute of Fiscal Studies reviewed the Coalition's record on poverty.[52] They found the data 'confusing'. Measures of relative poverty fell significantly. However, this was mostly because falls in median income reduced the poverty line rather than because of rises in the living standards of low-income households.

The Coalition government outlined strategies to reduce poverty in the long run. These were based on improving incentives to work, including a national living wage. This – along with the desire to simplify the system – lay behind the introduction of universal credit to replace different social security benefits.

The Conservative government of 2015 replaced the Child Poverty Act 2010 with the Welfare Reform and Work Act 2016. This abolished the targets to reduce poverty and the measure of poverty based on family income. The Social Mobility and Child Poverty Commission became the Social Mobility Commission. In December 2016, the government abolished the Child Poverty Unit set up in 2007 by the Labour government to coordinate action across Whitehall. Alarmed by this, Alison Garnham, chief executive of the Child Poverty Action Group, said: 'The threat level has escalated. We should be adding to our resources for getting children out of poverty, not diminishing them.'[53] However, a government spokeswoman said it was 'nonsense to suggest that the end of the standalone child poverty unit meant the government was not committed to its work'.

This exchange is symptomatic of the lack of consensus about what to do about poverty. A fissure has opened in our society. On the one hand, there are those who, like Mickelthwait and Wooldridge,[54] want to extend economic freedom further, curtail 'wasteful' welfare spending, and reduce democracy if it inhibits economic growth. On the other hand, there are those who yearn for the welfare state. Inevitably, the second group is on the back foot. The language of anti-poverty campaigners is problematic because it is based on resistance to dominant trends in society and uses concepts that fail to resonate with people. A meeting organised for the Trust by Compass concluded: 'Poverty campaigners have been running up the down escalator for decades trying to squeeze more and more out of the post war settlement and getting less and less in return.'[55]

We need an alternative, and that is the task of this book. It will start with the society we have and later compare it with the society we want.

Notes

[1] Webb, S. and Webb, B. (1909) *The break up of the poor law*, London: Longmans.

[2] Available from: www.webbmemorialtrust.org.uk/uncategorized/uk-poverty-and-inequality-workshop-report

[3] Watson, J. (2016) 'Is the third sector failing?', Webb Memorial Trust Supplement, *New Statesman*, 21 October.

[4] Bailey, O. (2016) 'Six principles for a new left narrative on poverty', Webb Memorial Trust Supplement, *New Statesman*, 21 October.

[5] Knight, B. (2015) *The society we want*, London: Alliance Publishing Trust and Webb Memorial Trust.

[6] Milner, A. (2015) 'Community action in an age of austerity: Meeting of 33 community activists at the Wilberforce Institute of Slavery and Emancipation', 27/28 October, unpublished report to the Webb Memorial Trust.

[7] Available from: www.jrf.org.uk/blog/talking-about-poverty-time-rethink-our-approach

[8] Webb, S. and Webb, B. (1912) *The prevention of destitution*, London: Longmans, Green and Company, p 12.

[9] Seymour, D. (2009) *Reporting poverty in the UK: A guide for journalists*, York: Joseph Rowntree Foundation, p 13.

[10] Runciman, W.G. (1966) *Relative deprivation and social justice: A study of attitudes to social inequality in twentieth-century England*, Oakland: University of California.

[11] Townsend, P. (1979) *Poverty in the United Kingdom*, London: Allen Lane and Penguin Books, p 31.

[12] Mack, J. and Lansley, S. (1983) *Breadline Britain: The findings of the television series*, London Weekend Television.

[13] Shildrick, T. and MacDonald, R. (2013) 'Poverty talk: How people experiencing poverty deny their poverty and why they blame "the Poor"', *The Sociological Review*, 61(2): 285–303.

[14] Callan, S. (2015) 'The poverty of the UK poverty measure', *The Spectator*, 25 June.

[15] Levitas, R., Pantazis, C., Fahmy, E., Gordon, D., Llloyd, E. and Patsios, D. (2007) *The multi-dimensional analysis of social exclusion*, Bristol: Department of Sociology and School for Social Policy, Townsend Centre for the International Study of Poverty and Bristol Institute for Public Affairs, University of Bristol, January. Available from: www.poverty.ac.uk/definitions-poverty/social-exclusion

[16] Sen, A. (2001) *Development as freedom*, Oxford: Oxford Paperbacks.

[17] Gordon, D. (2006) 'The concept and measurement of poverty', in Pantazasis, C., Gordon, D. and Levitas, R. (eds) *Poverty and social exclusion in Britain*, Bristol: Policy Press, p 32.

[18] Unwin, J. (2013) *Why fight poverty?*, London: London Publishing Partnership, p vii.

[19] MacDonald, R. and Shildrick, T. (2013) 'In poverty and in work', Webb Memorial Trust Supplement, *New Statesman*, 22 March.

[20] Westen, D. (2008) *The political brain: The role of emotion in deciding the fate of the nation*, New York: PublicAffairs.

[21] Marquand, D. (2014) *Mammon's kingdom: An essay on Britain now*, London: Penguin UK, p 184.

[22] Horton, T. and Gregory, J. (2009) *The solidarity society: Fighting poverty in an age of affluence*, London: Fabian Society and Webb Memorial Trust.

[23] Coates, D. (2012) *From the Poor Law to Welfare to Work: What have we learned from a century of anti-poverty policies?*, London: Smith Institute and Webb Memorial Trust.

[24] Hudson, J. and Lunt, N., with Hamilton, C., Mackinder, S., Meers, J. and Swift, C. (2016) 'Exploring public attitudes to welfare over the longue durée:

Re-examination of survey evidence from Beveridge, Beatlemania, Blair and beyond', *Social Policy & Administration,* 50(6): 691–711, DOI: 10.1111/spol.12256.

[25] Volmert, A., Gerstein Pineau, M. and Kendall-Taylor, N. (2016) *Talking about poverty: How experts and the public understand poverty in the United Kingdom*, Washington, DC: FrameWorks Institute.

[26] Webb, S. and Webb, B. (1909) *The break up of the poor law*, London: Longmans.

[27] William Beveridge Letter to the editor of the *Spectator*, 17 May 1956, page 14. Available from: http://archive.spectator.co.uk/article/18th-may-1956/14/letters-to-the-editor

[28] Reeves, R. (2014) 'Rachel Reeves's Clement Attlee memorial lecture: full text'. Available from: www.newstatesman.com/politics/2014/05/rachel-reevess-clement-attlee-memorial-lecture-full-text

[29] Rowntree, S. and Lavers, G.R. (1951) *Poverty and the welfare state*, London: Longman.

[30] Crosland, A. (1956, 2nd edition 2006) *The future of socialism*, London: Constable & Robinson.

[31] Available from: http://news.bbc.co.uk/onthisday/hi/dates/stories/july/20/newsid_3728000/3728225.stm

[32] Coates, D. (2012) *From the Poor Law to Welfare to Work: What have we learned from a century of anti-poverty policies?*, London: Smith Institute and Webb Memorial Trust.

[33] Krugman, P. (2007) 'Confessions of a Liberal', *New York Times*, 18 September.

[34] Titmuss, R. (1951) *Essays on the welfare state*, London: Allen and Unwin.

[35] Kincaid, J.C. (1973) *Poverty and equality in Britain: A study of social security and taxation*, Harmondsworth: Penguin, p 10.

[36] Abel-Smith, B. and Townsend, P. (1965) *The poor and the poorest: A new analysis of the Ministry of Labour's Family Expenditure Surveys of 1953–4 and 1960*, Occasional Papers on Social Administration no 17, London: Bell.

[37] Hood, A. and Oakley, L. (2014) 'The social security system: Long term trends and recent changes', IFS Briefing Note BN156, Institute of Fiscal Studies.

[38] The goals of the Mont Pelerin Society are included on the society's website. Available from: www.montpelerin.org.

[39] Cockett, R. (1994) *Thinking the unthinkable: Think-tanks and the economic counter-revolution, 1931–83*, London: Harper Collins.

[40] Covington, S. (1997) *Moving a public policy agenda: The strategic philanthropy of conservative foundations*, Washington, DC: National Committee for Responsive Philanthropy.

[41] Murray, C. (1984) *Losing ground: American social policy 1950–1980*, New York: Basic Books.

[42] Taylor-Gooby, P. (1985) *Public opinion, ideology, and state welfare*, London: Routledge & Kegan Paul.

[43] Golding, P. and Middleton, S. (1978) 'Why is the Press so obsessed with welfare scroungers?', *New Society*, 26 October; Golding, P. and Middleton, S. (1982) *Images of welfare*, Basingstoke: Macmillan.

[44] Coates, D. (2012) *From the Poor Law to Welfare To Work: What have we learned from a century of anti-poverty policies?*, London: Smith Institute and Webb Memorial Trust, pp 45–6.

[45] Coates, D. (2012) *From the Poor Law to Welfare To Work: What have we learned from a century of anti-poverty policies?*, London: Smith Institute and Webb Memorial Trust.

[46] Knight, B. (2008) *Child poverty in the north east of England*, Newcastle: Association of North East Authorities.

[47] Hills, J. (2004) 'The last quarter century: from new right to new labour', in Glennerster, H., Hills, J., Piachaud, D. and Webb, J. (eds) *One hundred years of poverty and policy*, York: Joseph Rowntree Foundation.

[48] Blair, T. (1999) 'Beveridge revisited: A welfare state for the 21st century', in Walker, R. (ed) *Ending child poverty: Popular welfare for the 21st century*, Bristol: Policy Press, p 16.

[49] Waldfogel, J. (2010) *Britain's war on poverty*, New York: Russell Sage Foundation.

[50] Joyce, R. and Sibieta, L. (2013) *Labour's record on poverty and inequality*, London: Institute of Fiscal Studies, 6 June. Available from: www.ifs.org.uk/publications/6738

[51] Bell, K. and Streilitz, J. (2011) *Decent childhoods: Reframing the fight to end child poverty*, Newcastle: Webb Memorial Trust, p 15.

[52] Joyce, R. and Sibieta, L. (2015) *The Coalition's record on poverty and inequality*, Institute of Fiscal Studies, 23 March. Available from: www.coalitioneconomics.org/uncategorized/the-coalitions-record-on-poverty-and-inequality/

[53] Available from: www.theguardian.com/society/2016/dec/20/fears-after-government-abolishes-civil-services-child-poverty-unit

[54] Wooldridge, A. and Micklethwait, J. (2014) *The fourth revolution: The global race to reinvent the state*, London: Penguin UK.

[55] Lawson, N. (2017) 'Ten steps to a society without poverty', unpublished report by Compass to the Webb Memorial Trust.

TWO

The society we have

The June 2016 referendum on whether to leave or remain in the European Union exposed the divisions in British society. Among various fault lines – political, demographic, social and economic – the starkest revelation was the collapse of trust between the political class and the people. Trust is the most basic building block of society and without it, it is almost impossible to move forward. For many, the decision to leave the European Union was a wake-up call to examine the state of British society. That is what this chapter sets out to do.

A deepening gloom

The gloom that descended on people and organisations concerned about social developments caused by the 2008 financial crisis, and made worse through austerity policies, has now reached crisis point. Hardly a week goes by without a report telling us how bad poverty is.[1] Topics include the growth in homelessness, the use of foodbanks, cuts to public services, falling wage rates, the record numbers of the working poor, the plight of refugees, and the likely rise in child poverty rates over the next five years. In the background, there is the sense of a deeply divided society where inequality has reached unsustainable proportions.

The continual barrage of bad news is itself another form of social malaise. The Trust asked Michael Orton of Compass to consider the theme of insecurity and his report, *Something's not right*, was published in 2015.[2] Having reviewed the evidence on social attitudes, housing, work, finances and health, he concluded that the UK is an insecure society in which 'fragmentation, discontinuity and inconsequentiality create a sense of flux, rather than solidity, and temporariness dependent on short term utility not permanence'.

Orton found that insecurity extends beyond people who have trouble making ends meet and permeates society.

The Trust also asked Neil McInroy to review evidence from the work of the Centre for Local Economic Strategies. In his report he notes:

> In my 25 years of working in the field of local economic development and regeneration, the situation has probably never been as bad. With little appetite for greater use of redistribution and/or re-mobilisation of the national welfare state or targeted social policy, we are left with an inadequate general rising economic tide to solve the scourge of poverty.[3]

The crisis has been a long time coming. While many of us were surprised by the result of the referendum, perhaps we shouldn't have been. A succession of reports – notably Brian Robson's 1994 forensic review of the limitations of area-based regeneration policies[4] – has highlighted the ineffectiveness of government policies in building a social infrastructure that would create a sense of common purpose and ensure the fruits of growth are shared fairly. A 2005 report based on interviews with directors of 15 leading charitable foundations suggested that they felt powerless in the face of continuing poverty, rising inequality, falling social capital and the rise of political extremism.[5] More recent reports suggest that the situation has become hopeless. John Harris, who has spent much of the past six years interviewing people from all over the UK, has noted that 'we are living in a country so imbalanced that it has effectively fallen over'.[6] George Monbiot has recently written of the '13 impossible crises that humanity faces'.[7]

The progress paradox

While acknowledging these problems, we need to heed the 'progress paradox' – a correlation between progress and pessimism. Peter Kellner, formerly president of polling company YouGov, notes how prosperity and pessimism tend to go hand in hand:

> The official statistics are clear. Our generation is better off, safer and destined to live longer than our parents' generation – and probably than any preceding generation. True, living standards in Britain and many other countries have stalled in the past few years, but this doesn't invalidate the larger truth.[8]

Larry Elliot writes in *The Guardian* of 21 April 2014:

> Britain is a richer, healthier, better educated and more tolerant country than it was 70-odd years ago. Life expectancy has risen by well over a decade; university education is no longer for a tiny elite; incomes adjusted for inflation are four times higher than they were at the end of the second world war; the number of people in owner-occupation has more than doubled; people no longer live in homes without baths and inside toilets.[9]

Statistics show that median equivalised household income has more than doubled since 1977 so that today's experience of relative poverty is very different from that of 40 years ago.[10] In *The progress paradox*, Gregg Easterbrook draws upon three decades of wide-ranging research to show that almost all aspects of Western life have vastly improved in the past century – and yet today most people feel that little progress has been made.[11]

Part of the explanation for this is 'negativity bias'. Threats have a greater effect on our psychological state than do neutral or positive things.[12] This bias makes it hard to reach balanced conclusions, and particularly to acknowledge progress. In *Future perfect*, Steven Johnson comments on newspapers' tendency to lead with bad news. This 'might be a good strategy for selling papers, but it necessarily skews our collective sense of how well we are doing as a society. We hear about every threat or catastrophe, but the stories of genuine progress get relegated to the back pages, if they run at all'.[13] Journalist Simon Jenkins has suggested that a Martian tuning into a radio broadcast would assume that Britain is a failed state.[14]

An earlier Trust publication, *The society we want*, showed that a negative outlook is a recipe for failure when it comes to social development. To make progress, we need a balanced assessment of both the assets and the deficits of our society. The next sections look systematically at our position in respect of four important variables that affect a good society: the economy, the public sector, civil society and poverty.

The economy

We live in a rich country. In terms of assets, Britain is the fifth richest country in the world behind the US, China, Japan and Germany.[15] In terms of gross domestic product (GDP), the UK has the fifth largest national economy in the world.[16] The service sector dominates the economy, contributing around 78 per cent of GDP. The financial services industry is particularly important, and London is the world's largest financial centre.

All governments since the Second World War have pursued growth as a key part of their economic strategy. In public speeches, our last three prime ministers have all stressed the importance of growth. At the 1994 party conference, when Gordon Brown was shadow chancellor of the exchequer, he set out Labour's approach: 'Labour will create the virtuous circle of investment, growth and improvements in our health and public services.'[17] David Cameron said that 'growth was vital' and his government had an 'incredibly active' growth strategy.[18] Theresa May stresses that driving growth 'up and down the country – from rural areas to our great cities' will be a priority, with a focus on 'rewarding hard-working people with higher wages'.[19]

Despite growth, the economy is commonly regarded as fragile.[20] The UK has the worst recent productivity record of any G7 country bar Italy. The balance of payments deficit is 7 per cent of GDP and the budget deficit 4 per cent of GDP. The Office of Budget Responsibility estimates the total public sector debt at £1.6 trillion while predicting it will rise to £1.7 trillion by 2020. A Trades Union Congress (TUC) report has found that unsecured household debt (including consumer credit and student loans, but excluding mortgages) rose to £319 billion in the third quarter of 2015 – a record high, and well above the 2008 total of £290 billion just before the financial crisis.[21]

Fears that the 2008 financial crisis will recur are never far from the surface. At Davos in 2016, William White, chair of the OECD's review committee, warned that 'debts have continued to build up over the past eight years and they have reached such levels in every part of the world that they have become a potent cause for mischief'.[22]

Growing inequality presents a further risk. Christine Lagarde, managing director of the International Monetary Fund, has long suggested that the gap between rich and poor could have 'tragic' consequences for the global economy,[23] and it is a recurring agenda item for the World Economic Forum. In the UK, financial journalist Stewart Lansley sees the main causes of inequality as the worship of shareholder value, the deregulation of banking, the bonus culture, the disappearance of middle-income jobs, the consumption culture, growing levels of debt and the housing bubble. He concludes, as others have done, that current levels of inequality are unsustainable and have done untold damage to our economic prospects.[24]

One of the most pernicious signs of inequality is a labour market that offers lavish rewards to people at the top while leaving many other people struggling. The High Pay Centre notes that the median pay of a chief executive of a FTSE100 company in 2015 was almost £4 million, while the median pay for the working population was £28,000.[25] The Trust supported the Child Poverty Action Group (CPAG) to develop a project called 'Britain at work'. Their report draws attention to the issues of stagnant or falling wages, rising prices, use of zero-hours, short-term or temporary contracts, self-employment, the impact of ᴄomation, tax credit cuts and universal credit work incentives. Added to this, the International Labour Office in Geneva notes that (in Europe as a whole) 'labour protection has generally decreased since 2008 when the global financial crisis started'.[26] This has led to the development of a 'precariat', people in low-paid, low-status, insecure jobs with few prospects, combined with an economy that has become increasingly informal.[27] This 'precariat' has grown rapidly over the past decade, with one TUC estimate suggesting one worker in ten is part of it.[28] It's particularly prevalent among young people. Resolution Foundation research shows that 77 per cent of 16–20 year olds were in low-paid jobs in 2015, up from 58 per cent in 1990; while the corresponding figures for 21–25 year olds were 40 per cent in 2015 and 22 per cent in 1990.[29] The Resolution Foundation also predicts that people in the bottom third of the income distribution will see their real incomes fall in the years ahead.[30]

The consequences for society are serious because, as the CPAG study shows, our experience of work is a key determinant of our health and happiness. Participatory research has shown that five factors make for good jobs: sufficient pay, job security, paid holidays/sick leave, a safe working environment and supportive line management.[31] According to the British Attitudes Survey, while 92 per cent of people think that job security is either important or very important, only around two-thirds of workers, 65 per cent, feel that they have this in their job.[32]

Suggestions for addressing this include creating more interesting jobs, developing a basic citizens' income and planning for leisure. Others have suggested investment in community cooperatives and social enterprises as a way of ensuring fairer distribution of resources. Ed Mayo, secretary general of Co-operatives UK, says: 'we need to ensure what develops is an economy that works for everyone. The co-operative sector, which is giving people a say over their work, shops and local areas is looking strong for the future and points the way'.[33] Although the cooperative sector is one of the fast-growing segments of the economy, alternative approaches to society and the economy have made little headway because of the obsession with economic growth. This obsession notwithstanding, there are good reasons to think it may soon have to be abandoned.

Moreover, we have to face the fact of the limits of growth. In 2014 *The Guardian* quoted fund manager Jeremy Grantham in its Sustainable Business section: 'People simply do not get the point that you can't have sustainable growth forever. You can have sustainability forever, or growth for a few years.' The idea is not a new one. As long ago as 1972, a book called *The limits to growth*[34] published the results of computer simulations of what would happen under various scenarios where exponential economic and population growth were combined with finite resources. The authors concluded that if present growth trends in population, industrialisation, pollution and food production continue, the limits to growth will be reached sometime in the next 100 years. In 2004, the authors updated the book and found their initial hypothesis vindicated by events, with climate change the most significant element of 'overshoot'.

Similarly, John Fullerton of the Capital Institute in the US argues that we are breaching safe ecological operating zones (emissions production, biodiversity). The root cause is our economic system: 'The universal patterns and principles the cosmos uses to build stable, healthy, and sustainable systems throughout the real world can and must be used as a model for economic-system design.'[35] He proposes what he calls regenerative capitalism. Under the present system, he argues, resources are put in service of the economy and then finance decides how the elements and products of the economy are allocated. He suggests a reversal of this arrangement: finance places itself at the service of the economy.

Succeeding governments, then, have placed their bets on economic growth as a means of ensuring prosperity and wellbeing. This idea will no longer do, first because the proceeds of that growth have not been distributed fairly. In addition, the limits to growth outlined above mean that attachment to economic growth, and to the notion that wellbeing depends on income and the ability to consume, will become less and less tenable.

The public sector

Just as we live in a rich country, we live in a country with a highly developed system of government. Divided into central government, local government and around 40 government-owned trading businesses (for example Ordinance Survey and the Met Office), the organisations that conduct government business are known collectively as the 'public sector'.

As seen in Chapter One, the public sector emerged triumphant from the postwar settlement. The public mood was one of 'rights not charity', exemplified by government minister Nye Bevan's remark as he launched the second reading of the National Health Service Bill in the House of Commons on 30 April 1946, "I believe we ought to have left hospital flag days behind."[36] Social planning and the provision of social services were to be done by the public sector on the principle that activities and services would be accountable to the electorate through parliament.

Radical changes to the organisation of government occurred during the 1980s. A swathe of legislation – the Education Act 1988, the Housing Act 1988, the Local Government Finance Act 1988 and the National Health Service and Community Care Act 1990 – enabled the contracting out of public services to the private and voluntary sectors. In line with the philosophy of 'new public management', the key role of government was to purchase rather than deliver public services. The rationale, explained in Osborne and Gaebler's bestselling 1992 book *Reinventing government*, was to introduce an entrepreneurial spirit into the operation of the public sector.[37] The approach has been followed by both Conservative and Labour governments ever since.

Research by the Institute of Fiscal Studies shows that over the second half of the 20th century government spending fluctuated between around 35 per cent and 45 per cent of national income, growing in real terms at an annual average rate of 2.7 per cent between 1948–49 and 1999–2000.[38] The first decade of the 21st century continued to see sustained increases in public spending, aggravated by the financial crisis of 2008 and the associated recession. To address the resulting deficit, the Coalition government and the new Conservative government have increased taxes and kept total public spending relatively flat in real terms, resulting in spending as a share of national income falling dramatically between 2009–10 and 2019–20.

These policies have meant cuts to public sector budgets. Figure 2.1 shows where these cuts have fallen in the years 2010–11 to 2015–16.

The scale of the budget cuts has meant reductions in services. The most dramatic are at local authority level. A *Financial Times* survey in July 2015 found that: 'Across Britain, services have been abandoned and entitlements altered as the chancellor has conducted one of the developed world's most effective exercises in deficit reduction.' It found that local authority budgets had been cut by £18 billion in real terms since 2010 – with at least another £9.5 billion expected by the end of the decade.[39] A study commissioned by the Joseph Rowntree Foundation suggested: 'The poorest communities and residents are being hardest hit and those least able to cope with service withdrawal are bearing the brunt.'[40]

These findings raise key questions about the capacity of the public sector to deliver a good society in the coming years, particularly in light of the uncertainty created by Brexit. As a Deloitte's review of the fiscal landscape puts it: 'Whitehall and the UK's regulatory bodies face a complex challenge in assessing how the detailed regulatory landscape will need to change as the UK leaves the EU, and what the implications will be for public bodies subject to EU directives.'[41]

Government capacity is further eroded by distrust of politicians. This has been thrown into sharp relief by the EU referendum, but it is not a new problem. IPSOS Mori has been running the same survey on trust in key professions since 1983. At no point during that period have more than a quarter of the public ever trusted politicians to tell the truth. Worries about people's disengagement from politics are not new either. At the time of the 2001 election, Hayes and Hudson found a worrying disengagement from politics when only 59 per cent of those eligible to vote did so.[42] At the time, Meg Russell suggested that 'we have lost sight of what politics is for', which in turn suggests a 'deep underlying cultural malaise that needs to be addressed'.[43] The all-time

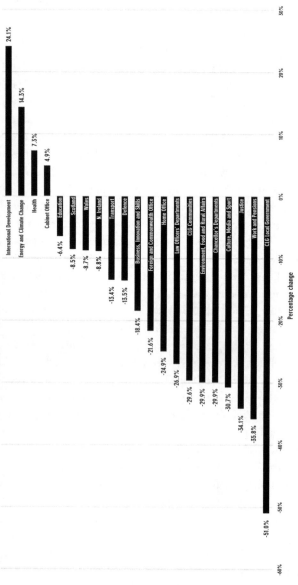

Figure 2.1: Real-time percentage cuts in departmental expenditure limits 2010–11 to 2015–16

International Development 24.1%
Energy and Climate Change 14.3%
Health 7.3%
Cabinet Office 4.9%
Education -6.4%
Scotland -8.5%
Wales -8.7%
N. Ireland -8.8%
Transport -13.4%
Defence -13.5%
Business, Innovation and Skills -18.4%
Foreign and Commonwealth Office -21.6%
Home Office -24.9%
Law Officers' Departments -26.9%
CLG Communities -29.6%
Environment, Food and Rural Affairs -29.9%
Chancellor's Departments -29.9%
Culture, Media and Sport -30.7%
Justice -34.1%
Work and Pensions -35.8%
CLG Local Government -51.0%

Percentage change

Note: CLG Local Government, Scotland and Wales budgets are adjusted for the effects of council tax benefit localisation and the business rates retention policy. The Defence budget includes the special reserve in 2015–16.
Source: HM Treasury, Public Expenditure Statistical Analyses 2015. Available from: www.gov.uk/government/statistics/public-expenditure-statistical-analyses-2015

low in trust in politicians was recorded in 2009 in the wake of the expenses scandal, when only 13 per cent said they trusted politicians.[44]

The chronic problem of dissatisfaction with conventional politics has let in space for the rise of extremism. Again, this is not new. With its tough line on crime and anti-immigration policies, the British National Party (BNP) proved attractive to some voters in local elections in May 2003. The BNP won three council seats in the northern town of Burnley – the scene of riots fuelled by racial tension in summer 2001. Overall, the BNP averaged 18 per cent in the 19 results contested nationwide – the far right's best showing since the late 1970s. Martin Jacques noted that 'fascism and an ugly racism are alive', but 'not since the 1930s has the threat … of a turn towards barbarism been so great in the west'.[45]

Since then, populism has been on the rise across the US and Europe. Inglehart and Norris have conducted an impressive analysis of the reasons, focusing particularly on factors of economic insecurity and cultural backlash. They find that the main driver is cultural backlash, 'especially among the older generation, white men, and less educated sectors, who sense decline and actively reject the rising tide of progressive values, resent the displacement of familiar traditional norms, and provide a pool of supporters potentially vulnerable to populist appeals'.[46] The rise of the UK Independence Party (UKIP) has had a marked effect on British politics. Although electoral success in the UK has eluded it, it gained a foothold in the European Parliament elections of 2014, and has obtained its core objective of obtaining Britain's exit from the European Union.

Civil society

In the late 1980s and early 1990s both the communist order and apartheid were dismantled, partly because of pressure for change from ordinary citizens. This prompted the rediscovery of the idea of 'civil society', dating from the Enlightenment, as a space between the state and the market where citizens and their institutions can produce social solidarity and influence public affairs. This led to a new Washington

Consensus, which involved a growing private sector, a diminishing role for the state, and an expanding civil society where citizens would play a greater role in determining their own affairs. Many hoped that the new world order would produce freedom, prosperity and solidarity.

However, Ralf Dahrendorf argues in *After 1989* that it is impossible for more than two of these to coexist in society at any one time and that freedom and prosperity have prevailed at the expense of solidarity.[47] Other studies seem to confirm this. Robert Putnam showed the decline of community in America, with people becoming increasingly disconnected from their relationships with family, friends and neighbours and withdrawing from civic life.[48] A comparable British study demonstrated the decline of collective action through reduced membership of churches, trade unions and civic associations.[49] The voluntary sector has also declined as an independent force. The final report of the Independence Panel of the Baring Foundation in 2014 noted: 'Under successive governments, the voluntary sector has increasingly become seen as a contractual arm of the state, without an independent mission or voice, interchangeable with the private sector.'[50]

At the same time, there are many voluntary and community organisations that provide a progressive view of the world, and are working towards a good society without poverty. These include the Joseph Rowntree Foundation, Child Poverty Action Group and Church Action on Poverty, among many others. The End Child Poverty campaign, for example, has more than 100 member organisations, including the train drivers' union Aslef, Barnados, the National Union of Teachers and the National Society for the Prevention of Cruelty to Children (NSPCC). More broadly, a review of UK progressive society (outside party politics), undertaken by Compass and the New Economics Foundation (NEF), identified 160,000 organisations, employing 800,000 people and with an annual turnover of £39 billion.[51]

However, the Compass–NEF review also identified weaknesses. First among these is lack of a shared vision. While the review noted strong and overlapping values – equality, democracy, social justice – there is no agreement on what these values mean in practice, resulting in an absence of focus and priority. Such considerations have caused leading commentators on civil society, such as Michael Edwards, to conclude that despite their numbers, the influence of civil society organisations is limited.[52] Moreover, community organisations that work from the bottom of our societies are fragile and can easily fizzle out.

There are examples which show that this trend is not universal and give grounds for some optimism. Over the course of 25 years Citizens UK has built a power base among citizens to work on issues affecting local communities, such as the living wage, jobs, housing, safety, refugees and the participation of excluded minorities. The Trust research suggests that there is much energy at community level to contribute to society, but it is difficult to connect this to established systems of governance. In a sense, this is another symptom of popular disenchantment with politics. Neither communities nor their elected leaders seem able to communicate with each other.

No review of civil society, however brief, can be complete without recognising that social media has brought wholesale changes to the way that we organise our lives and relationships. A Trust-sponsored review of current social trends found that technology and social media 'is the big driver of change'.[53] Social media enables civic actors to organise in ways of their own choosing. We have seen the rise of Kickstarter (for creative projects) and Avaaz (for people-powered politics), and the development of popular hashtags on Twitter such as #BringBackOurGirls and #WeAreHere.

While social media has great potential for organising for good, it has a corresponding potential for propagating hate. In 1990 Mike Godwin, then a law student, formulated 'Godwin's Law': 'as an online discussion grows longer, the probability of a comparison involving Nazis or Hitler approaches one'.[54] Academic John Suler has studied the 'online disinhibition effect' in which people tend to be more spiteful and less restrained online than in person.[55] That this has had its effect on politics was easy to see during the 2016 American election, when vindictiveness and personal attacks became prevalent. This behaviour is increasingly common in the UK and, according to journalist Jamie

Bartlett, is 'ruining politics'. 'Twitter storms, online spats and insults are making it impossible to talk to one another and reach the compromises on which public life depends.'[56] At the same time this hate may not be visible to many users of Twitter because, as the empirical studies cited by Ian Harford show, people of different views rarely interact on Twitter since we tend to follow people whose views we agree with.[57]

Poverty

The 2016 annual report *Monitoring poverty and social exclusion*, produced by the New Policy Institute for the Joseph Rowntree Foundation, showed that there were 13.5 million people living in low-income households in 2014–15, representing 21 per cent of the UK population. This proportion, based on the criterion of falling below 60 per cent of the median income, has barely changed since 2004–05.[58] Since median incomes have stagnated over much of this period, we can conclude that there has been little recent progress in reducing poverty whether a relative or an absolute measure is used.

What *has* changed over the past decade or so is the composition of people affected by poverty. Figure 2.2 compares the numbers of people in different groups in poverty in two different years: 2004–05 and 2014–15. The big changes are the increases in poverty among working families and those living in private rented accommodation.

Figure 2.3 goes into more detail about the prevalence of poverty among different groups. A glance at the chart shows that poverty tends to be concentrated among four different groups: people without work, people from various black and minority ethnic backgrounds, single parents and disabled people. It also shows the importance of housing in making poverty worse, particularly for people in the social and privately rented sectors.

A recent report by the Joseph Rowntree Foundation noted:

> The level of poverty in the UK is shameful. This should be a place where everyone can live a decent, secure life. Instead, 13 million people – half of whom are in a working family – are living without enough to meet their needs.[59]

Figure 2.2: People in poverty after housing costs in different groups in 2004–05 and 2014–15 (millions)

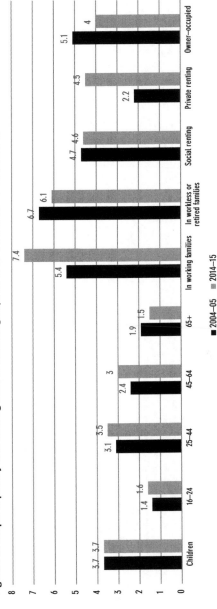

Note: The data for poverty by age is a three-year average.
Source: New Policy Institute (2016) Monitoring poverty and social exclusion. Available from: www.jrf.org.uk/report/monitoring-poverty-and-social-exclusion-2016

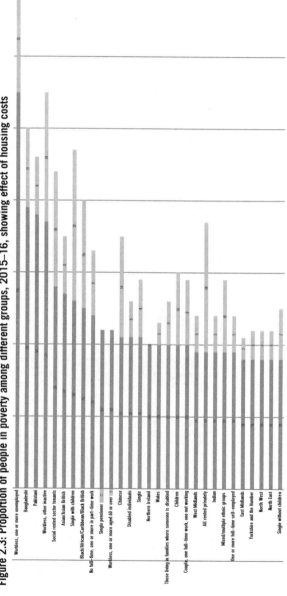

Figure 2.3: Proportion of people in poverty among different groups, 2015–16, showing effect of housing costs

Source: Household Below Average Income Series 1994–95 to 2014–15. Available from: www.gov.uk/government/statistics/households-below-average-income-199495-to-201516

Figure 2.3 (continued): Proportion of people in poverty among different groups, 2015–16, showing effect of housing costs

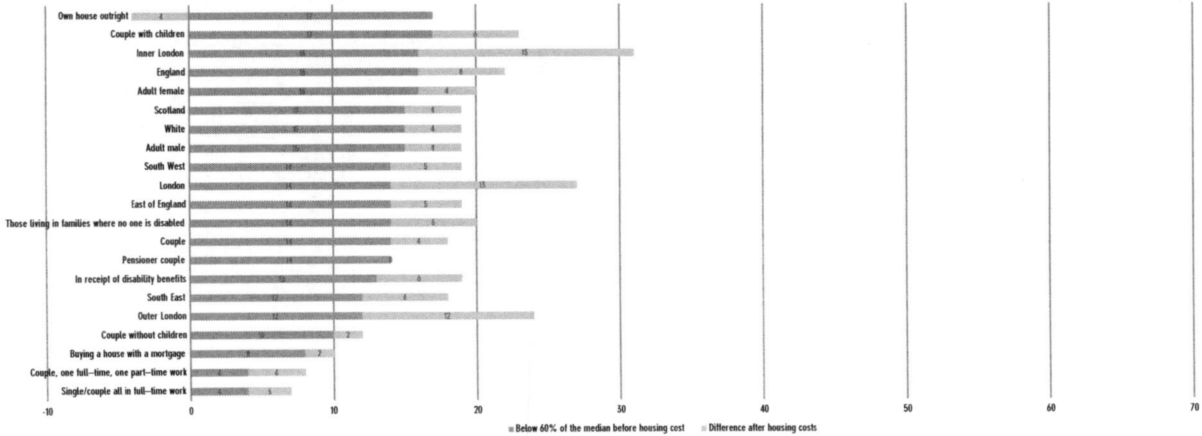

Below 60% of the median before housing cost   Difference after housing costs

Source: Household Below Average Income Series 1994–95 to 2014–15. Available from: www.gov.uk/government/statistics/households-below-average-income-199495-to-201516

The literature on the consequences of poverty suggests that it causes much damage: to individuals who are poor themselves, to children born to parents with low incomes whose life chances are thereby reduced, and to society generally. The 2014 report of the Living Wage Commission gives many examples.[60] The American Psychological Association has also collected evidence of the harmful effects of poverty on many dimensions of life, including health, educational attainment, use of leisure and psychosocial wellbeing.[61]

The reality of how poverty affects children's lives became evident during a programme the Trust developed in the North East. In 2011, the Trust supported Children North East to run a conference called 'Child poverty: definitely not a thing of the past'. As part of the preparations, 517 children were given disposable cameras and asked to photograph what poverty meant to them; this resulted in 11,000 pictures. Focus group discussions were held involving 133 children, and a group of children from a low-income area of Newcastle was supported to write and perform a play called *A day in the life of Hope*.

This process highlighted the emotional damage that poverty does to children. The children typically used expressions of 'embarrassment' and 'shame'. "I am embarrassed to bring my friends home", said one. "I am too ashamed of our house to invite my friends for a sleepover", said another. Money is always a problem: "If you don't have money, you can't do anything"' Children rarely go anywhere: "It's £240 for a family to go to Alton Towers", and "All your money is spent on bus fares". Staying at home is no fun either because "Loads of people around here are horrible, graffiti, fights and talk about bad stuff"'. There is nowhere to play: "You can't play in the park because it's covered in rubbish, then you play in the street and adults get annoyed." And the area is run-down: "Our area looks really bad with all the 'to let' signs, like no one wants to live there." Other work preparing for the conference revealed that one in six of the thousands of poor children in the North East had contemplated suicide.

As regards diminished life chances between the generations, there appears to be a cycle.[62] Parents who live in poverty bring up their children in conditions of poverty. These children tend to become poor adults in turn and *their* children grow up in poverty. There is a close correlation between incomes of parents and achievements of children.[63] Every year a child spends in poverty increases the chances that they will fall behind the level of their classmates by the age of 18. Such children are also less likely to receive supportive parenting because their parents' poverty means they commonly suffer from 'anxiety, depression, and irritability', leading them to be 'punitive, inconsistent, authoritarian, and inconsiderate towards their children'. Driscoll and Nagel show that poor children are twice as likely to have stunted growth, iron deficiency and severe asthma. [64]

Poverty puts children at greater risk of dying before their first birthdays than mothers smoking during pregnancy. Overall, children growing up in poverty are not only more likely to suffer poor health and do less well at school but are also more likely to become the next generation of adults at risk of unemployment and long-term poverty.

While most of the literature on the effects of poverty focuses on the effect on individuals or families, there is also evidence of harmful effects on wider society. A 2008 report aiming to give 'an estimate of the extra cost to selected public services of the existence of child poverty' put the costs of child poverty in the UK to public expenditure at between £11.5 billion and £20.7 billion a year. This took into account personal social services (for example, provision of support to children because of abuse or neglect), healthcare, education, housing, police and criminal justice, fire and rescue, local environmental services (for example, street cleaning, maintenance of parks and open spaces), and area-based programmes (for example, the Neighbourhood Renewal Programme).[65] More recently, the Joseph Rowntree Foundation has estimated the overall costs of poverty at £78 billion per annum.[66]

Poverty is a major cause of social tensions dividing people within a country.[67] Groups in Britain who have been 'left behind' by rapid economic change and feel cut adrift from the general current of life in the UK – people on low incomes with no qualifications and low skills – were the most likely to support Brexit.[68]

Society is drifting

Why has this happened? As noted in the earlier part of this chapter, social questions have been neglected at the expense of the pursuit of material prosperity – despite the failure of the economic system to distribute gains in such a way as would satisfy the majority. Notwithstanding increasing criticism of the economic growth paradigm, we are reluctant to abandon it. We have drifted into what is sometimes called the 'Washington Consensus', in which the market is the arbiter of all things, government responsibility for social provision is reduced, and civil society takes on – or attempts to take on – that responsibility.

Three bestselling books in the past few years have produced powerful criticisms of the current system, particularly in relation to the role of the market and the consequent rise in inequality. Thomas Piketty demonstrated that the returns on capital have persistently exceeded the returns on labour, leading to long-term increases in inequality.[69] Richard Wilkinson and Kate Pickett showed how inequality damages society.[70] Finally, Michael Sandel revealed how markets have permeated every aspect of life, damaging our sense of value.[71] Almost everyone – at most points on the political spectrum – believes that the neoliberal philosophy has run its course. This includes economists at the International Monetary Fund who believe that the philosophy has been oversold.[72] These things matter and affect ordinary people's lives.

There are many areas where the current system is failing ordinary people. Planning is a good example. The Trust commissioned the Town and Country Planning Association (TCPA) to review the English system of land use planning. It concluded:

> The planning system was invented to help provide a good home, for everyone, in a healthy, thriving place. But in the last few decades something has gone badly wrong. Instead of having people's welfare as its priority, nowadays the English planning system puts economic growth above all else. What has this achieved? All over the country working people can't afford to

buy a home. People on benefits are forced to move hundreds of miles away because there are no affordable rented homes where they live. And local councils are unable to refuse permission for developments that they know will harm their communities.[73]

The TCPA suggested that the UK is a rich society that is poorly organised. To make progress, it is vital for us to bring back a sense of utopia that focuses on 'meeting people's needs for homes, green spaces, and attractive towns, cities and villages'. Through its #planning4people campaign, the TCPA has brought together a powerful coalition of like-minded people and organisations to work to change planning for the better.

How do we achieve the changes we need? Government has neither the means nor the credibility to provide a solution. The purely economic approach to prosperity has failed, and people are increasingly looking for forms of wellbeing that are not solely material. Policy makers and experts on the one hand, and communities at the sharp end of a divided and uneasy society on the other, are unable to communicate with each other. All this indicates the need for a new approach.

The first and most important step is to admit our confusion. This is vital if we are to make progress. As former Greek finance minister Yanis Varoufakis puts it:

Nothing humanises us like *aporia* – that state of intense puzzlement in which we find ourselves when our certainties fall to pieces ... and when the *aporia* casts its net far and wide to ensnare the whole of humanity, we know we are at a very special moment in history.[74]

Stewart Lansley has identified four conditions for the kind of transformation we need: severe economic shock; the intellectual collapse of the existing model; a loss of faith by the public in the existing system; and a ready-made and credible alternative. The first three have already come about. What is missing is a coherent, ready-made and widely endorsed alternative that would command public support.[75] Developing such an alternative is the task of the next chapter.

Notes

[1] Knight, B. (2015) *The society we want*, London: Alliance Publishing Trust and Webb Memorial Trust.

[2] Orton, M. (2015) *Something's not right*, London: Compass and Webb Memorial Trust, p 13.

[3] McInroy, N. (2015) *Forging a good local society: Tackling poverty through a local economic reset*, Manchester: CLES and Webb Memorial Trust, p 3.

[4] Robson, B., Bradford, M. and Parkinson, M. (1994) *Assessing the impact of urban policy*, London: Stationery Office.

[5] Knight, B. (2005) *Social justice, poverty reduction and inclusive communities: The role of independent charitable trusts and foundations*, Report to the Barrow Cadbury Trust.

[6] Harris, J. (2016) 'We are living in a country so unbalanced that is has effectively fallen over', *The Guardian*, 24 June.

[7] Monbiot, G. (2016) 'The thirteen impossible crises that humanity now faces', *The Guardian*, 25 November.

[8] Kellner, P. (2015) 'Analysis: The curious link between prosperity and pessimism', *YouGov*, 25 November. Available from: https://yougov.co.uk/news/2015/11/10/curious-link-between-prosperity-and-pessimism .

[9] Elliot, L. (2014) 'We need a new Beveridge for 21st-century Britain', *The Guardian*, 21 April.

[10] Available from: www.ons.gov.uk/peoplepopulationandcommunity/personalandhouseholdfinances/incomeandwealth/bulletins/nowcastinghouseholdincomeintheuk/2015-10-28

[11] Easterbrook, G. (2003) *The progress paradox: How life gets better while people feel worse*, New York: Random House Incorporated.

[12] Cacioppo, J.T., Cacioppo, S. and Gollan, J.K. (2014) 'The negativity bias: Conceptualization, quantification, and individual differences', *Behavioral and Brain Sciences*, 37: 309–10.

[13] Johnson, S. (2012) *Future perfect: The case for progress in a networked age*, New York: Riverhead Books, p XIV.

[14] Jenkins, S. (2016) 'Here is the news: it's usually bad and that's bad for us', *The Guardian*, 21 April.

[15] Jefford, K. and Parmenter, C. (2015) 'World wealth: Britain crowned fifth richest country in the world behind US, China, Japan and Germany', CityA.M., 3 November.

[16] Central Intelligence Agency (2017) *World factbook*. Available from: www.cia.gov/library/publications/the-world-factbook/geos/uk.html

[17] Brown, G. (1994) 'Shadow Chancellor's speech', Labour Party Conference, Blackpool, September. Available from: http://www.britishpoliticalspeech.org/speech-archive.htm?speech=278

[18] BBC (2011) 'David Cameron defends economic growth policy', 1 October. Available from: http://www.bbc.co.uk/news/uk-politics-15138606

[19] Smithard, T. (2016) 'Theresa May's new strategy: Growth everywhere, not just the north', *Total Politics*, 2 August. Available from: www.totalpolitics.com/articles/news/theresa-mays-new-strategy-growth-everywhere-not-just-north

[20] Elliott, L. (2016) 'The fragile UK economy has a chance to abandon failed policies post-Brexit', *The Guardian*, 17 July.

[21] TUC (2015) 'Record high for family debt shows that we don't have a recovery that works for all', 8 January. Available from: www.tuc.org.uk/economic-issues/labour-market-and-economic-reports/economic-analysis/britain-needs-pay-rise/record

[22] Inman, P. (2016) 'Fears grow of repeat of 2008 financial crash as investors run for cover', *The Guardian*, 20 January.

[23] Iwing, J. (2016) '"Inequality is feeding protectionism", I.M.F. chief warns', *New York Times*, 5 April.

[24] Lansley, S. (2012) *The cost of inequality: Why economic equality is essential for recovery*, London: Gibson Square.

[25] High Pay Centre (2017) 'Fat cat Wednesday', 4 January. Available from: http://highpaycentre.org/blog/fat-cat-wednesday-2017

[26] Torres, R. (2015) *World employment and social outlook, 2015: The changing nature of jobs*, Geneva: International Labour Office.

[27] Standing, G. (2011) *The precariat: The new dangerous class*, London: Bloomsbury Academic.

[28] O'Connor, S. (2016) 'One in 10 UK workers in insecure employment, says TUC', *Financial Times*, 16 December.

[29] Clarke, S. and D'Arcy, C. (2016) *Low pay Britain*, London: Resolution Foundation.

[30] Resolution Foundation (2016) 'Renewed living standards squeeze is set to be greater in this parliament than the last', 24 November. Available from: www.resolutionfoundation.org/media/press-releases/renewed-living-standards-squeeze-is-set-to-be-greater-in-this-parliament-than-the-last

[31] Stuart, F., Pantz, H., Crimin, S. and Wright, S. (2016) *What makes for decent work? A study with low paid workers in Scotland*, Oxford: Oxfam.

[32] British Social Attitudes Survey 33. Available from: www.bsa.natcen.ac.uk/latest-report/british-social-attitudes-33/work.aspx

[33] Mayo, E. (2016) 'Co-operative Economy 2016 report shows 'resilience' in the face of uncertainty'. Available from: www.thenews.coop/106138/sector/retail/co-operative-economy/

[34] Meadows, D.H., Meadows, D.L., Randers, J. and Behrens, W. (1972) *The limits to growth*, New York: Universe Books.

[35] Fullerton, J. (2015) 'Regenerative capitalism: How universal principles and patterns will shape our new economy', April, Capital Institute, Page 8. Available from: https://bsahely.com/2016/04/22/life-capitalism-one-life-science-to-rule-them-all/

[36] See http://hansard.millbanksystems.com/commons/1946/apr/30/national-health-service-bill

[37] Osborne, D. and Gaebler, T. (1992) *Reinventing government: How the entrepreneurial spirit is transforming government*, Reading, MA: Adison Wesley Public Comp.

[38] IFS (2105) 'Total UK public spending', 28 September. Available from: www.ifs.org.uk/tools_and_resources/fiscal_facts/public_spending_survey/total_public_spending

[39] Gainsbury, S. and Neville, S. (2015) 'Austerity's £18bn impact on local services', *Financial Times*, 19 July.

[40] Hastings, A., Bailey, N., Bramley, G., Gannon, M. and Watkins, D. (2016) *The cost of the cuts: The impact on local government and poorer communities*, Joseph Rowntree Foundation. Available from: www.jrf.org.uk/sites/default/files/jrf/migrated/files/Summary-Final.pdf

[41] Deloitte (2017) 'The state of the state 2016–17'. Available from www2.deloitte.com/uk/en/pages/public-sector/articles/state-of-the-state.html

[42] Hayes, D. and Hudson, A. (2001) *Basildon: The mood of the nation*, London: Demos.

[43] Russell, M. (2005) 'Must politics disappoint?', *Fabian Society*, 21 March.

[44] Available from: www.ipsos-mori.com/researchpublications/researcharchive/3685/Politicians-are-still-trusted-less-than-estate-agents-journalists-and-bankers.aspx

[45] Jacques, M. (2002) 'The new barbarism', *The Guardian*, 9 May.

[46] Inglehart, R.F. and Norris, P. (2016) *Trump, Brexit, and the rise of Populism: Economic have-nots and cultural backlash*, Cambridge, MA: Harvard Kennedy Business School, p 4.

[47] Dahrendorf, R. (1997) *After 1989: Morals, revolution and civil society*, New York: Springer.

[48] Putnam, R. (2000) *Bowling alone*, New York: Simon and Schuster.

[49] Knight, B. and Stokes, P. (1996) *The deficit in civil society in the UK*, Birmingham: Foundation for Civil Society; Hall, P. (1999) 'Social capital in Britain', *British Journal of Political Science*, 29: 417–61.

[50] Independence Panel (2015) *An independent mission: The voluntary sector in 2015*, London: Baring Foundation, p 3.

[51] Orton, M. (2016) 'Creating a shared vision', Webb Memorial Trust Supplement, *New Statesman*, 21 October.

[52] Edwards, M. (2014) 'When is civil society a force for social transformation?', *Open Democracy*, 30 May. Available from: www.opendemocracy.net/transformation/michael-edwards/when-is-civil-society-force-for-social-transformation

[53] Lawson, N. (2016) 'The context for a world without poverty', Compass. Available from: www.compassonline.org.uk/wp-content/uploads/2016/11/The-Context-for-a-World-Without-Poverty_DRAFT_V2-6.pdf

[54] Amira, D. (2013) 'Mike Godwin on Godwin's Law, whether Nazi comparisons have gotten worse, and being compared to Hitler by his daughter', *New York Mag*, 8 March. Available from: http://nymag.com/daily/intelligencer/2013/03/godwins-law-mike-godwin-hitler-nazi-comparisons.html

[55] Suler, J. (2004) 'The online disinhibition effect', *Cyberpsychology & behavior*, 7(3): 321–26.

[56] Bartlett, J. (2017) 'Gove's "snowflake" tweet is symptomatic of the nastiness that's ruining politics', *The Guardian*, 21 January.

[57] Harford, I. (2016) *Messy: How to be creative and resilient in a tidy-minded world*, London: Little, Brown.

[58] Tinson, A., Ayrton, C., Barker, K., Born, T.B., Aldridge, H. and Kenway, P. (2016) *Monitoring poverty and social exclusion 2016 (MPSE)*, New Policy Institute, 7 December. Available from: www.jrf.org.uk/report/monitoring-poverty-and-social-exclusion-2016

[59] Joseph Rowntree Foundation (2016) *We can solve poverty*. Available from: www.jrf.org.uk/report/we-can-solve-poverty-uk

[60] Living Wage Commission (2014) *Working for poverty: The scale of the problem of low pay and working poverty in the UK*. Available from: www.edf.org.uk/living-wage-commission-working-for-poverty/

[61] American Psychological Association. Available from: www.apa.org/pi/families/poverty.aspx

[62] Gordon, D. (2011) *Consultation response: Social mobility and child poverty review*, Policy Response Series No 2, Poverty and Social Exclusion in the UK.

[63] Magnuson, K. (2013) 'Reducing the effects of poverty through early childhood Interventions', *Fast Focus*, 17 (University of Wisconsin).

[64] Driscoll, A. and Nagel, N. (2007) *Early childhood education, birth-8: The world of children, families and educators* (4th edition), Boston: Allyn & Bacon Longman.

[65] Bramley, G. and Watkins, D. (2008) *The public service costs of child poverty*, York: Joseph Rowntree Foundation.

[66] As reported by the BBC, and available from www.bbc.co.uk/news/uk-36937516

[67] Available from: www.poverties.org/effects-of-poverty.html

[68] Goodwin, M. and Heath, O. (2016) 'Brexit vote explained: Poverty, low skills and lack of opportunities', Joseph Rowntree Foundation, 31 August. Available from: www.jrf.org.uk/report/brexit-vote-explained-poverty-low-skills-and-lack-opportunities

[69] Piketty, T. (2013) *Capital in the 21st century*, Cambridge, MA: Harvard University Press.

[70] Wilkinson, R. and Pickett, K. (2009) *The spirit level: Why equal societies almost always do better*, London: Allen Lane.

[71] Sandel, M.J. (2012) *What money can't buy: The moral limits of markets*, London: Penguin.

[72] Ostry, J.D., Loungani, P. and Furceri, D. (2016) 'Neoliberalism: Oversold?', *Finance & Development*, June, 53(2), pp 38–41.

[73] The #Planning4People manifesto is available from: www.tcpa.org.uk/planning4people

[74] Varoufakis, Y. (2011) *The global minotaur*, Chicago: University of Chicago Press Economics Books, p 1.

[75] Orton, M. (2016) 'Creating a shared vision', Webb Memorial Trust Supplement, *New Statesman*, 21 October.

THREE

The society we want

This chapter describes what people want from their society. It uses the first of the three questions that framed the Trust's research: what is a good society without poverty?

The chapter starts by explaining why deciding what we want as a society matters. Next comes a brief description of the key findings from the research, followed by an explanation of the Trust's approach and a description of the multiple methods used to reach conclusions. Finally, the chapter sets out what the Trust has learned from the various studies undertaken.

Why we should decide what we want

We need to decide what kind of society we want because, unless we know where we are going, we will almost certainly land somewhere else. In *Ill fares the land*, Tony Judt suggests that big normative questions have fallen off the agenda:

> We no longer ask of a judicial ruling or a legislative act: is it good? Is it fair? Will it help bring about a better society or a better world? Those used to be *the* political questions, even

if they invited no easy answers. We must learn once again to pose them.[1]

The idea of the good life is central to the way we construct meaning in our lives. What we believe in, how we act, and the institutions we build all contribute to who we are. The key text here is the famous 1977 essay by Berger and Neuhaus, which examined the importance of 'mediating structures' such as family, church, workplace and neighbourhood in enabling people to live good lives and to develop a healthy society.[2]

The importance of these mediating structures has declined over the past half-century and this appears to be symptomatic of a deeper shift. Society has moved from one predominantly concerned with production to one concerned with consumption, so that the present appears unrecognisable from the past. Zygmunt Bauman has described this as the process of moving from 'solid modernity' to 'liquid modernity'. While in the past we saw ourselves as 'pilgrims' in search of deeper meaning in a stable world, we now see ourselves as 'tourists' in search of multiple but fleeting social experiences. It is now harder to construct a durable sense of ourselves; we tend to live a fast life in a kaleidoscope of relationships.[3]

This has created a crisis of meaning in our lives, and consumerism has filled the void. As Neal Lawson puts it in his 2009 book *All consuming*, 'Shopping has been emotionally, culturally and socially grafted onto us'. He also says that for many it is an addiction that fails to satisfy us: 'Turbo-consumerism is the heroin of human happiness.'[4] An extreme form of such consumerism can be found in the 'celebrity culture' in which famous individuals transform their fame into product brands, which the public then consumes. In emulating celebrities, ordinary people use the 'selfie', posting their photos on social media to display the illusion that life is 'all about me'. Such developments were foreseen 50 years ago by Guy Debord in his 1967 *Society of the spectacle* in which 'authentic social life has been replaced with its representation'. Debord argues that the history of social life can be understood as 'the decline of being into having, and having into merely appearing'. This condition is the 'historical moment at which the commodity completes its colonization of social life'.[5]

The price is a soul sickness at the heart of our society which breeds deep insecurity and unhappiness for many, while violating the basis in nature on which our species depends.

Principles of a good society

The Trust's aim is to articulate the principles of a good society. To do this, it has undertaken many different types of research to locate a small number of key ideas that find resonance across many different people. The goal is to produce five principles to compare with neoliberalism's five principles (free markets, small state, low tax, individual liberty and big defence).

The Trust realises that this is a complex undertaking and simple answers can only be provisional. It has used theoretical research, empirical surveys, professional reports, focus groups and participatory research. While results are based on many perspectives, they emphasise the views of people who have experienced poverty.

The wording of the five principles has been hammered out in numerous ways during the research. The wording is not perfect but, as will be shown later, the 'tyranny of perfection' is an enemy of progress towards the society we want.

The five principles of a good society are:

1. We all have a decent basic standard of living.
2. So we are secure and free to choose how to lead our lives.
3. Developing our potential and flourishing materially and emotionally.
4. Participating, contributing and treating all with care and respect.
5. And building a fair and sustainable future for the next generations.

One underlying concept that links the five principles is the idea of 'community'. Below are four quotations from different focus groups, each of which expresses this in a slightly different way:

'A good society would be one in which everybody lived together in a harmonious community where everyone is treated fairly.' (Focus group for benefit recipients)

'I think a good community with people who are friendly and who pull together, and maybe have the same ideals and goals in life, is the basis for a good society.' (Focus group for people on low incomes)

'A good place to be in, a decent community.' (Focus group for people on medium incomes)

'I think that for there to be a good society, people should be working together to achieve a common goal and feel included in the process – having a sense of belonging and sharing.' (Focus group for people on high incomes)

The five principles, set out very simply here, result from a long process. Later in the chapter both the empirical findings and the participatory research on which these principles are based will be described in more detail. Since the process of reaching them tells us as much about who we are and how we live as the principles themselves, a description of how they were arrived at now follows. Since the task is a normative one, the process is inevitably difficult. It involves overcoming many barriers, some of which lie in our own attitudes, behaviours and assumptions.

Our habits of thought are barriers

Although there is near-universal agreement that we need new ways to give meaning to our lives and the society that we live in, there are three commonly occurring patterns of thought that prevent us from finding them.

The first barrier is the idea that developing a new way of thinking about the world and the purpose of society is simply a matter of changing the words while keeping the substance. Bret Davidson points out that the prevailing narrative runs deep into our cultural patterns, and reframing it needs to address how people construct their reality.[6] At the Trust workshop on communications mentioned in Chapter One, communications consultant Deborah Mattinson concluded: 'You need to start where the public are at; don't think you will get them to think the way you do about an issue.'[7]

The second barrier to developing a solution is starting with the problem. This often relies on what George Lakoff has called 'negative framing'.[8] Statements that are phrased negatively – in terms of getting rid of a problem – commonly produce the opposite of what is intended because the mention of the subject focuses attention on it. Lakoff's example is 'don't think of an elephant'. Robert Fritz's work on creativity has shown that if we try to solve a problem, we often reinforce it, which is why dieting so often fails.[9] Negative framing often attacks the symptoms rather than the causes of a problem. As seen in Chapter One, poverty is a symptom of economic mismanagement, unequal structures and inadequate state intervention. Rather than starting with the problem, we need to devise a system that delivers what we want. As Carl Rogers put it:

> Another great challenge of our times ... is to develop an approach that is focused on constructing the new, not repairing the old; that is designing a society in which problems will be less frequent, rather than putting poultices on those who have been crippled by social factors.[10]

The third barrier is thinking that there is a technocratic solution which only academic research can find. If you establish a correlation between a problem such as poverty and a factor that appears to drive it, says this kind of argument, you can frame a policy to reduce its influence and thus solve, or at any rate greatly diminish, the problem. In the complex, non-linear world of social relationships, we cannot treat problems in this way, because to identify a simple cause among many other contributory factors is well-nigh impossible. Recommendations from reports conducted by think tanks or universities rarely address such complexity.

The moral imagination

To make effective use of evidence, we need to employ an explicitly normative frame using what John Paul Lederach has called 'the moral imagination'.[11] This entails an inclusive process in which relevant people use divergent thinking to mould the society they have into the future they want.

Lederach notes that it requires creative processes that are more akin to art than to traditional processes of development. As the pursuit of professional excellence in society has emphasised the technology, techniques and skills of process management, he suggests, we have too often lost a sense of the art: 'our approaches have become too cookie-cutter like, too reliant on what proper technique suggests as a frame of reference, and as a result our processes are too rigid and fragile'.[12]

The use of the moral imagination is in a sociological tradition that derives from C. Wright Mills and his book *The sociological imagination*, published in 1959.[13] Mills admonished his social science colleagues for becoming obsessed with narrow, discipline-based technical applications and esoteric language that obscures the point that the key task for sociologists is to connect social history and personal biography and to imagine better futures. Following Mills, Lederach defines the job of moral imagination as being: 'To imagine responses and initiatives that, while rooted in the challenges of the real world are, by their nature, capable of rising above destructive patterns and giving birth to that which does not yet exist.'[14]

Lederach's approach builds on a distinction between two types of thinking – 'convergent' and 'divergent' – deriving from the work of psychologist Liam Hudson.[15] In convergent thinking, the solution to a problem is found by bringing material from a variety of sources to bear on a problem, in such a way as to produce the 'right' answer. In divergent thinking, the solution is found by radiating outwards from any given stimulus. There is no right answer but a new configuration of phenomena that did not exist before.

Such processes need to be both creative and inclusive. With some notable exceptions, the campaigns to end poverty in the UK are neither of these things. Much of the writing about poverty is dull, technocratic and exclusionary. The idea of creativity is a more fruitful starting point and is more likely to engage people. The starting point for a good society is in our moral imagination.

Theory of a good society

There is an extensive literature on how to understand a good society going back at least to the time of Plato and Aristotle. Some of the literature is considered in *The society we want*.[16] A glimpse at it is sufficient to show a bewildering complexity of views. Even so, boiled down to essentials, there are two dominant and opposing traditions, centred on freedom and equality. Fernand Braudel observes that if it were possible to record the whole of European history on a computer and then search for the problem that comes up most often, it would be liberty – 'or rather liberties', for liberty is generally at odds with the liberties, or privileges, of particular groups.[17] Where these are asserted successfully, they encroach on the liberty of all and inequality makes its appearance.

While this is of course an oversimplification, Mark Rosenmann's excellent review of the 'common public good' shows that this bifurcation of thought stretches back into history and colours almost all writing about the good society.[18] Mickelthwait and Wooldridge trace it through history, beginning with Thomas Hobbes and his search for a social contract to bring order to human affairs. They move on to the influence of John Stuart Mill and his pursuit of liberty through to Beatrice Webb and her quest for social security, finishing with Milton Friedman and his desire for freedom.[19] Throughout the history of the past 400 years, it is possible to observe the conflicting dynamic between freedom and equality. While freedom has exercised a powerful pull over the politics of the left since the 18th century, more recently it has come to be associated with parties on the centre-right, with their emphasis on the individual and rejection of state interference. The tension between the two forces is sharply exposed, for example, in the conflict between the philosophies of laissez-faire and planning in the last years of the 19th century. It is evident in the current polarisation of political views in Europe.

It is axiomatic that a good society cannot be a divided society. Division leads to groups insisting on their views more strongly since they see them as under threat – a 'we are right' syndrome, which diminishes the plurality of civil society and marginalises minority views. It also produces negative stereotyping of the 'other', which leads in turn to a polarisation of politics into extreme positions which simply entrench the divisions and create a gulf across which it is impossible to communicate – except by shouting. Finally, these developments lead to a collapse in trust, a growing sense of insecurity, and a consequent increase in the force of hate. All this was evident in 2016, first during the referendum on Britain's membership of the European Union and then in the American presidential election.

There is nothing new in this downward spiral. Mark Mazower's revisionist study of Europe in the 20th century shows how the break-up of the Holy Roman Empire unleashed two brands of hatred that are still with us: Islamophobia and antisemitism.[20] He suggests that *Les Trentes Glorieuses* between 1945 and 1975 were a brief respite in European affairs and we are now reverting to normality. Whether or not we accept this view, it's a reminder that seeing government provision of social welfare *as a right* has a relatively short history. Since we are living in that period of history, it's difficult for us to see beyond it, easy to think that it will always be so. Mazower reminds us that the progress of history is as often cyclical as it is linear.

At the end of this brief foray into the theory of a good society, we can conclude that, while theory helps us to clarify the competing tendencies at the heart of European thought and their long-running effects on our societies, it is of little assistance in providing a compass for us to find our way. We do, however, learn that there are no easy answers and everything is contested. At the same time, when we look more deeply, using an empirical lens, we can find much that is common between us regardless of the outward complexion of our political views. While there is plurality, there is also scope for compromise.

The method

The study used many methods to try and understand this. It took an evolutionary approach, using the results of one phase of work to frame the next so that the findings were built up on an iterative 'create and adjust' basis. First, the Trust commissioned a population survey of 2,000 people from YouGov to identify attitudes to a good society and poverty. Following this, 12 focus groups were held, drawn from various subgroups in the YouGov sample. The results were then analysed and key hypotheses identified, which were tested on a much larger sample of 10,000 people.

This study unearthed the key factors that people feel make up a good society and these were used as the basis for further research work. The research commissions were of two main types. First, several participatory research exercises were conducted in which groups affected by poverty were asked to develop their views of a good society without poverty and how this might be attained. The views of the different groups were drawn on to formulate the five principles for a good society. Second, professional organisations were commissioned to address themes arising from these population studies.

The second strand of research involved studies by think tanks and professional researchers. These included work on child poverty, transport, housing, security, welfare, planning, civil society and fairness commissions. Funded organisations were encouraged to arrange meetings with relevant individuals and organisations to disseminate and discuss the work. A key part of the programme has been to promote meetings of community activists, people from voluntary organisations, public sector workers, businesspeople and others to build a constituency to take the work forward. In all these activities, the Trust has been careful to remain above party politics. It has supported the All Party Parliamentary Group on Poverty, which has been a useful way of encouraging conversations between civil society and parliamentarians of all kinds.

Although the Trust has tried to be as comprehensive and as creative as it could, while also getting to grips with as much of the relevant literature as possible, it would be the first to recognise the limitations of its approach. The goal is to set out a series of hypotheses that others can take on. The good society is as much in the making of it as in the finished product. As Neal Lawson put it in a report for the Trust:

> The Good Society is one that *we* create, it cannot be something done to us. Hope comes from the insight that the way we make things and make things happen in the 21st Century allows the means and ends of a good society to be aligned. *'You can't go around building a better world for people. Only people can build a better world for people. Otherwise it's just a cage',* wrote Terry Pratchett in *Witches Abroad*. Nowhere is this truer than the ending of poverty, a process that now can and must involve the poor being their own agents of change.[21]

What was learned from empirical surveys

The empirical results demonstrate the importance of plurality. The fact that the study is dealing with a normative question about a good society means that there can be different opinions. Such variation is not a problem so long as compromise is seen as a source of strength not weakness; it is a central feature of a good society.

When it comes to a good society, the word that matters most is 'fairness'. Trust-sponsored surveys asked 10,112 adults over the age of 16 to say 'which one of the following phrases best describes what you would like Britain to be?' Answer options were:

- an 'everyone for themselves' society;
- a 'fair' society;

- an 'equal' society;
- 'UK PLC';
- don't know.

A majority (60.9 per cent) opted for a 'fair' society. The next most popular option was an 'equal' society (20.7 per cent). The other options were much less popular (7.0 per cent for 'UK PLC', 2.0 per cent for an 'everyone for themselves' society and the remaining 8.4 per cent 'don't know').

Early pilot studies and focus groups identified 17 qualities that people said were important for a good society. These were tested in the population survey from two angles: their importance and their presence. First, people were asked 'how important, if at all, do you think each of the qualities are for a "good society"?' Answer options were: 'very important', 'fairly important', 'not very important', 'not important at all' and 'don't know'. Second, people were asked 'how present, if at all, do you think that each of the following is in Britain today?' Answer options were: 'very present', 'fairly present', 'not very present', 'not present at all' and 'don't know'.

Figure 3.1 shows the percentages who said that each quality was 'very important' or 'fairly important' for a good society and the percentages who said that it was 'very present' or 'fairly present'.

It is noteworthy that all items score 74 per cent or above when it comes to importance, reflecting the fact that the items chosen had been identified as important in earlier stages of the research. What is striking is the variation between the different items and their rank order: eight of the nine items that score 90 per cent or above measure social qualities, such as security, safety and independence, rather than economic ones. The highest economic indicator, well-paid work, is ranked sixth, while prosperity comes twelfth. For most people, the good life is not about having a lot of money; it is about having enough to pay their way and occasionally enjoy a few luxuries. Both having well-paid work and the absence of poverty are important, largely because they help people to live fuller lives. There was a general

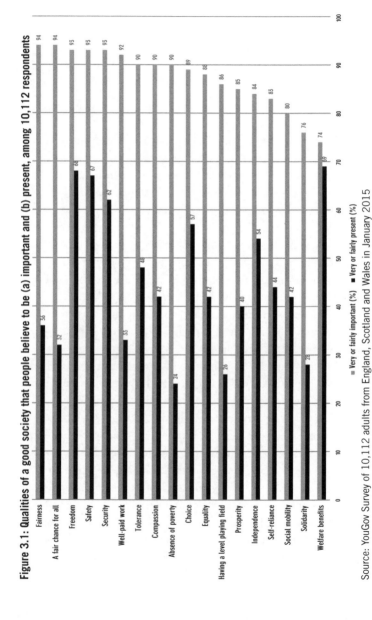

Figure 3.1: Qualities of a good society that people believe to be (a) important and (b) present, among 10,112 respondents

■ Very or fairly important (%)   ■ Very or fairly present (%)

Quality	Important	Present
Fairness	94	36
A fair chance for all	94	32
Freedom	93	68
Safety	93	67
Security	93	62
Well-paid work	92	35
Tolerance	90	48
Compassion	90	42
Absence of poverty	90	24
Choice	89	57
Equality	88	42
Having a level playing field	86	26
Prosperity	85	40
Independence	84	54
Self-reliance	83	44
Social mobility	80	42
Solidarity	76	28
Welfare benefits	74	69

Source: YouGov Survey of 10,112 adults from England, Scotland and Wales in January 2015

sense from the focus groups that material possessions matter less than community:

'I think a good society should place much less emphasis on material things. Is it a coincidence that since people have had more stuff and money "community spirit" is perceived to have reduced?'

'There is too much greed in the world and while we allow that, we will never make progress.'

At the same time, people want a balanced life:

'A good society should provide the opportunity to do well in life, realise ambitions, provide opportunities for work and ensure that everyone has a stake in society.'

We need to have a basic standard of living and to sort out the economic stuff first, and that puts people in a position to make a trusting, equal community.

Although some people see the idea of community as utopian, most people feel that Britain is at its best when we are 'together' in a venture such as the Olympics. As one focus group respondent put it: "When the crowd cheered on Mo Farah in the 10,000 metres as he won the gold, I thought 'yes, we really are in this together'." Such a community is not a static place; it is continually evolving through new communities such as social media, though it relies heavily on face-to-face contact. A retired focus group participant said: "I go to a day centre and we spend a lot of time talking and doing things together. It really lifts my spirits."

Many participants – particularly those in the discussion groups for new migrants and Asian people – talked at length about a desire for more cohesive communities. In the migrant group 'cohesion' means, in part, physical security and freedom from being victims of hate crime.

However, participants also talked at length about a sense of belonging and acceptance that comes from shared cultural and moral values. For some this means protecting the traditions of 'their' community; for others it means reaching out to others. An Asian participant noted: "The community centre is a great place where you can meet new people ... I've learnt a lot about myself and different cultures being here." However, some communities feel under attack and this can make them less willing to open up to other communities. A member of a black focus group noted:

'I'm not sure young people today have the same opportunities to "learn" about different heritages. We do "Black History Month" and we think that's ok to show that little bit of heritage to other communities. But I think a few years ago we were more willing to talk to other people. We've lost that a bit.'

The idea of community, which grounds people's identity, is underpinned by four key qualities: safety, tolerance, fairness and equality. Although people mean different things when they talk about these qualities, they form the basis for their place in the world, giving them the opportunity to develop and thrive.

There is widespread agreement that a good society should not have poverty in it. In focus group discussions, most agreed that there is no need for anyone to live in absolute poverty in a good society. A typical comment was: "I think if there are people in society living in poverty it is not a good one." However, in some groups people stressed that, as one participant put it, "It is inevitable that some people are going to be poorer than others". The issue of relative poverty divides people and many people believe that a society can still be a good one even if there is relative poverty. A participant spoke for many when she said: "Poverty is unlikely to be eliminated as someone will always be poorer than someone else but in a good society there should be a minimum standard of life and perhaps much less gap between the richest and poorest."

Analysis of the characteristics of survey respondents and their answers to questions allowed the identification of key groups in society based on their attitudes towards a good society and the role of poverty. A hierarchical cluster analysis found six groups, which were labelled based on their characteristics as 'idealists', 'libertarians', 'conservatives', 'realists', 'stoics' and 'disengaged'.

Idealists

'Idealists' are the group who are most moved by poverty and wish to do something about it. Idealists typically read *The Guardian*, vote Labour or Liberal Democrat, and are more prevalent in Scotland than other parts of the UK. They see the value of the welfare state and access to services. They are concerned about the consequences of social inequality and wish to improve the environment. They value tolerance and social mobility. For idealists, government action on poverty should mean that people in poverty live a life as close to normal as possible.

Idealists are more likely than other groups to see a gap between their views and the state of Britain. But they are optimistic that intervention could see improvements on issues such as education, hunger and mental health. They see government, employers and businesses as having an important role in this, while families have little role to play. Idealists form an estimated 12 per cent of the population.

Libertarians

For 'libertarians', the key quality is self-reliance. Poverty is the result of people's bad choices, and individuals and families are responsible for their own poverty. Libertarians typically vote Conservative; they are concerned about immigration and feel that it will increase poverty. There are, however, more important priorities than poverty, which typically ranks towards the bottom of what is important for them.

Libertarians feel that many people are over-dependent on the NHS and that welfare benefits should be linked to contributions. They agree that government should help people in poverty but only to stop them starving. Families, not the state, should have the main responsibility to help people who fall into poverty. For libertarians, Britain is a compassionate place but poverty is inevitable. They form 19 per cent of the population.

Idealists and libertarians are at the extremes of opinion when it comes to the issue of a good society without poverty. While idealists stress structure, libertarians stress individual agency. All other groups – 69 per cent of the population – fall between these two extremes. Being generally more moderate, they have fewer stand-out characteristics.

Conservatives

'Conservatives' are particularly concerned with 'fairness' and having a level playing field. They typically see choice and well-paid work as the keys to a good society. They are more likely than other groups to say that Britain is fair and secure and offers well-paid work, so they tend to be more content with the current condition of society.

Conservatives are likely to read the *Financial Times* or *The Times*. They are likely to say that other issues are more important than poverty and inequality, and that unemployed people should look harder for work because poverty is often due to people's choices. They would like to see less of a 'free handout culture' in Britain and tend to feel that some people are over-dependent on the NHS. Conservatives are the most prevalent group, forming 23 per cent of the population.

Realists

'Realists' are likely to read the *Daily Mirror* or the *Daily Record*. They typically see themselves as poorer than average and tend to be in classes D and E. They are most likely to vote Labour or UKIP and see structural causes for poverty. While most people see buying a second-hand car as 'normal', realists see this as a luxury. Realists worry that immigration is increasing poverty. They form 18 per cent of the population.

Stoics

'Stoics' see poverty and associated conditions as an inevitable part of a modern society. Despite that, they support the living wage. They feel that reducing the cost of living and providing affordable housing would ameliorate the worst effects of poverty.

Stoics tend to be characterised by the lack of strong opinions, though the idea of tolerance is very important to them. They feel that knowing people is the way to get on. They form 17 per cent of the population.

Disengaged

The final group is labelled 'disengaged'. They typically answer survey questions 'don't know'. They are prevalent among the 18–24 age group. They are more likely to live in London, be unemployed or a student, and read the *Sun* or *Star* newspapers. They are sceptical about schools being able to do much to reduce poverty. They form 10 per cent of the population.

This analysis shows that a strategy to develop a good society without poverty must take account of a wide variety of perspectives. There are also questions that are difficult to deal with. The surveys and focus groups uncovered the negativity and tensions that are at work in our society. Respondents who believe that people are responsible for their own poverty are, for example, particularly apt to criticise those on benefits. When people of this opinion come together for a discussion, they encourage each other, and the tone of the conversation tends to deteriorate into a process of blame. What follows is part of a dialogue among a focus group of people selected because they share the view that poverty is caused by people's bad choices:

> **Paul** (aged 36, head of retail): 'People find themselves in bad situations through bad choices. Why should society pay for it?'
> **Lewis** (aged 55, communications worker): 'They don't choose to be in need but they make bad choices then find themselves there.'

Mary (aged 75, living alone): 'Many disabled people work, they are not all looking for handouts.'

Johnny (aged 41, local government officer): 'If someone is fit to work, then they should have no choice but to be made to look for work.'

Mary: 'And it is our role in society – a good society – to help those who are in need the most, not those who choose to be in need.'

Paul: 'I don't believe that a perfectly healthy person in their 30s or 40s can be in need of support.'

Allan (retired army officer): 'How about forcing the feckless to take the burger-flipping job but top them up to a living wage rather than give them the dosh free?'

The research found that people with views like these tend to display feelings of insecurity and vulnerability in their own lives. Indeed, the more insecure a person feels inside, the more likely they are to project their negative emotions onto others, stereotyping them and scapegoating them for all the ills of society.[22] The findings fit well with Anna Freud's 'mechanisms of ego defence', in which people use unconscious processes to transfer their anxieties onto others to maintain their emotional homeostasis.[23] Such a process is more prevalent among people who suffer what psychiatrist R.D. Laing called 'ontological insecurity'. Migrants, minorities and people on benefits tend to become scapegoats for people who lack, to quote Laing, 'a centrally firm sense of one's own and other people's reality and identity' which arises from the experience of one's 'presence in the world as a real, alive, whole, and ... [temporally] continuous person'.[24] The importance of a sense of security is a key finding from our research.

Participatory research

Survey research, focus groups and consultations with civil society groups can take understanding only so far. The methods used so far cast people as 'respondents' or 'interviewees', implying that they have little control over the shape and control of the research. These are essentially 'supply-side' approaches to the issue of poverty. The Trust decided it needed to address the 'demand side' by providing an opportunity for individuals on low incomes to develop and express their own ideas. This involved research *with* rather than *on* individuals and is an important corrective to the tendency in the poverty lobby for professionals to speak for people in poverty, a practice that further marginalises people who are already marginalised. As part of the focus group research, people on benefits sometimes complained that it is patronising for political activists to use their adverse circumstances to campaign for the political changes that they want to see.

The method used was participatory research. This approach has a long pedigree, pioneered in the Global South during the 1970s by Rajesh Tandon and brought to the attention of the West by practitioners such as Robert Chambers and John Gaventa.[25] Though the approach is less well practised in the UK, the Trust could assemble for its work a good team of practitioners including Ghiyas Somra, Ruth Patrick and Dan Farley, Sara Bryson and Rys Farthing as well as Michael Orton.

In participatory research, people use their skills, knowledge and experience to devise their own framework, develop the questions and produce solutions. As Bennett and Roberts put it:

> Participatory approaches to research and inquiry into poverty recognise the particular expertise of people with experiences of poverty to put forward their own realities – and their right to do so – and can also make research more effective and improve its impact on policy.[26]

In allowing deeper conversations over a longer period, the method reveals the complexity of issues, drawing on subjective and emotional experience and enabling highly nuanced conclusions. The process is often chaotic, but it's free from the logic of theory, the division of ideology or the neat categories of social research. Rather than forcing 'either/or' answers to questions, it allows 'both/and' feelings to emerge.

Binary opposites drive people to conclusions that do not fit well with their feelings. People want freedom *and* security, collective approaches *and* individual ones. The participatory research suggests that a good society is based on conjunctions rather than disjunctions.

The open-ended nature of participatory research means that it is difficult to manage and requires a high level of facilitation skills. A critical part of the process is to build the confidence among participants so they believe they can engage in big ideas, and produce clear and concise results – using John Paul Lederach's view of the 'moral imagination', outlined above.

An ethos for working together was developed, based on seven key points:

- emphasising what we agree on (not points of disagreement);
- seeing cooperation and compromise as strengths (not weaknesses);
- being positive and focused (not just criticising, looking at negatives, discussing problems and being a talking shop);
- stepping outside organisational boundaries and seeing working together as a vital starting point not an optional afterthought;
- accepting a 'good enough' outcome (not insisting on individual ideological perfection);
- being curious about different views, listening and ensuring everyone has their say;
- acting with care, compassion and respect for each other.

Given that each group could choose its own topics and approaches, there was no guarantee that useful comparisons could be made between different groups. However, there was an impressive consistency in the themes and perspectives, which suggests a high degree of agreement about what people want. What follow are the main findings from four separate participatory exercises.

Children's voices

The work featured here was undertaken by children and young people. Over a three-year period the Trust supported several interlinked projects, including a conference in the North East of England, the production of a play by children, a photography project and an online game, together with a series of residential meetings in which children could develop and record their thoughts.[27]

The work culminated in a document called *Poverty ends now.*[28] Thirty-eight young people, drawn from five of the poorest wards in different cities in England, contributed to writing this based on the work of a wider group of 180 young people between 2012 and 2014. Children and young people did all the work. Though adults were on hand to offer guidance, they were careful not to control decisions. The name 'Poverty Ends Now' (PEN) was chosen because the young people felt that it was commanding, short, and catchy for social media purposes and because the PEN acronym matched what they were doing – writing.

To implement their findings, the children planned three national actions: a launch of their manifesto in parliament, tabling parliamentary questions and writing an evidence submission, and undertaking a national media campaign. The All Party Parliamentary Group on Poverty provided a forum for the national work. The children also planned six local actions based on the six themes that emerged as central to young people's concerns: decent incomes in Liverpool, affordable housing in London, equality at school in the North East, healthy food in Gateshead, feeling safe in Manchester, and public transport in Newcastle.

The final manifesto was clear and succinct. It was based on six principles:

1. A minimum standard of living, not just surviving, for every family in Britain.
2. An equal schools experience for all.
3. Affordable, decent homes for everyone.

4. Access to three affordable, healthy meals a day for every young person.
5. A feeling of safety within their communities and at home for everyone.
6. Affordable transport for all young people everywhere.

These principles were derived from the life experiences of the young people. Unlike many people who write about poverty, the young people 'tell it straight' based on their own authentic experience. In the box are excerpts from children's descriptions of what it's like to live on a low income in their neighbourhoods.

Children's descriptions of what it's like to live on a low income

On food banks: 'It's povvie. It's poverty. Like proper poverty ridden. Do you know what I mean? But at the end of the day, beggars can't be choosing. If you need the stuff, you need the stuff. You got to provide for your family, and that's the only way you can do it. You have to swallow your pride and deal with it.'

On housing: 'It's crap. Why do you think I go to the (youth club) coughing and sneezing at the same time?'

On personal hygiene: 'You don't know how bad it is having nits. People are like "there's things moving in your hair", and you're like "Ummm ... flies, they're flies".'

On neighbourhoods: 'How would you like to live in an area that's considered to be a dump?'

On the authorities: 'The worst thing about living in poverty is the way it gives others permission to treat you as if you don't matter.'

Deliberations leading to the manifesto reveal that children see things differently from adults. Their perception is more direct and concrete – focusing on immediate things like the lack of food in the fridge, the inability to go on school trips, or the embarrassment of bringing friends home to a flat with rising damp. Things that have little place in the poverty debate among adults, such as love from parents or caring for pets, are very important to children. Children lack the theoretical baggage that adults tend to carry, avoiding quibbles about issues such as the best definition of poverty. They also feel that whatever is wrong should be fixed now. The title of their manifesto, *Poverty ends now*, speaks to an immediacy that is rarely present in the policy debates of adults. As one of the children said: "It's the job of adults to fix things, and I don't understand why they talk about things but never seem to do them."

The difference in frameworks between adults and children produced one of the most valuable outcomes from the project. As one of the professional workers who facilitated the work of the young people commented in a project report: 'The strongest outcome was the democratic challenge the project posed those working in the "poverty" sector, locally and nationally and implicitly and explicitly.' In her report, she cited an event in Manchester:[29]

> You could see the decision makers present (from police commissioners to councillors to voluntary sector people) slowly coming around to the realisation that these young people were 'key stakeholders' (their words) in decisions they'd be making for a while now, and that their views were incredibly important.

All the local projects were successful in raising awareness about the value of young people's views. To take some examples, in Liverpool young people developed a play called *Brass Razoo*, which was performed to a full house in November 2014. Trade unions saw the potential of using the play to promote discussion of the issues and gave the group financial support to enable a second performance at a 1,000-person capacity theatre. In Manchester, the police commissioner began to work with the group of young people on issues ranging from sexual exploitation to park lighting. In the North East the group met every two weeks to discuss poverty and education. On the advice of their local MP the group conducted a questionnaire in their own schools and colleges to gather evidence about the impact of poverty in schools. They spoke to over 1,000 local young people, analysed the findings and organised a local evidence session with 60 regional decision makers. The group has now been offered funding by the North-East Child Poverty Commission to continue meeting over the next year to act as a shadow youth board of the commission as well as continuing their work on the manifesto priorities.

All local events engaged local councillors, MPs, teachers and others. They all attracted local press coverage. That young people used exciting ways of engaging people, such as plays and real-life examples, as opposed to traditional reports, helped to attract attention.

Nationally, the work raised awareness of the issues, though there is less evidence of lasting outcomes. *Poverty ends now* was launched on 15 October 2014 at the Houses of Parliament. Young people presented the report to a large audience of other young people and some MPs and peers, and engaged in a formal questioning of three MPs, one from each of the three main political parties. Although the event was highly successful and had a positive effect on the confidence of the young people, there was no sense that any further action would be taken. There is a risk that much effort can go into supporting events and actions of this kind, but that messages, while listened to at the time, have little effect on policy or practice. This raises the vexed question of participation and power: people may be able to take part in political processes, but it does not follow that they have any power to change things.

Black and minority ethnic voices

The second participatory research project was conducted by BRAP,[30] a charity that works on equalities. A total of 42 people took part in five working groups, each from a different cultural background – Asian, Black, multiple heritage, recent arrivals and White British.

A central finding from this work is that fulfilling interpersonal relationships are fundamental to people's wellbeing and sense of happiness. This is partly because relationships give people a sense of security:

'I would look after my mum first, because she's always been there for me when I've needed her … I know she always will be – whatever happens, at school or college – I know she'll love me and my brothers and sisters.' (Group of young people)

'As you get older you realise that having someone who cares about you is more important than all the things that you got hung up about before – the cars and the big house.' (Mixed race group)

Closely connected to being loved, many participants discussed the importance of being respected and the impact this has on people's self-esteem:

'Respect, for me, is one of the most important things. Respect for yourself, because a lot of people don't respect themselves, but when you respect yourself you'll respect other people.' (Mixed race group)

Participants felt that respect is central in a good society and its absence causes damage. This is invariably wrapped up in discussions about racism:

'Stereotypes are really damaging. I have been pulled over by police for running, like in my running gear with my brother, and asked what I was doing. It was stupid because it is like, "how are you going to ask me what I am doing if I am running and you can clearly see that?" It's obvious they just see you as "a black man".' (Black group)

'It annoys me how based on ethnicity you are called different things even if you are doing the same thing, say for instance holding a knife: for black people you are violent criminals, for

Muslims it is dangerous terrorists and for white people they are misunderstood, or just playing a game. It's obvious who they think is part of society and who isn't.' (Black group)

Each group quickly reached the conclusion that we do not live in a fair society – one in which everyone has access to the same opportunities as everyone else without fear of discrimination. The society that they want is based on five principles:

1. **'We won't judge you because of who you are.'** A good society will take active steps to ensure people aren't discriminated against in public life (education, employment, health, the criminal justice system, and so on). Discrimination can take many forms and can be on many grounds, including class. Simply obeying equality laws isn't enough: we need to change the way society privileges some sections of itself.

2. **'Your problems are our problems.'** Life is hard for a lot of people. They're not academic, didn't get much out of school, and are now finding it difficult to get a job. Perhaps they're stuck living at home. Perhaps they have health problems and have no one to talk to. A good society shows compassion. It can't help everyone and it won't solve people's problems for them. But it will say, 'you're worth investing in'. Because it recognises that people aren't stupid, or too lazy to get a job, or just need to go out and make some friends. It recognises that people are part of a system whose rules they didn't create.

3. **'We'll make work worthwhile.'** People value work. It provides independence and a sense of self-reliance. Productive work gives people a feeling of accomplishment. As such, work should provide people with the resources to ensure they can afford the basics in life and take part in the opportunities a fair society offers.

4. **'We'll help you find a place where you feel accepted.'** A good society will ensure people can access other people with similar interests, concerns and values. This is partly about ensuring such opportunities are available – that there are places, programmes and

events people can go to. And it's partly about ensuring people aren't restricted in accessing these things because their horizons are too narrow or because there are cultural or societal pressures preventing them from doing so.

5. **'We're happy if you fulfil your dreams – whatever they might be.'** The only measure of success is whether people reach the goals they set themselves. A good society will certainly stretch people if they don't think they're able to achieve all they're capable of. But it won't push particular narratives or agendas. It won't reward only monetary success. It won't idolise only the wealthy. It won't portray society as a competition.

Organised groups of poor people

The third example is participatory work with three groups of people living in poverty – Dole Animators in Leeds, Thrive in Teesside and ATD Fourth World in London – facilitated by Ruth Patrick and Dan Farley. This group was different from the others in that it produced pictures of its work with the assistance of Dan Farley.

Pictures for two of the groups are shown in Figures 3.2 and 3.3. It is striking that both display a remarkable similarity to the five concepts developed by Michael Orton in *Secure and free*, though at no time did the workshops mention this project. This suggests that the agreement over key solutions was completely organic and that there is much scope for building consensus.

What people want from their society is modest, as reflected in the picture from Thrive in Teesside. They are not seeking flashy cars, expensive phones or fashionable clothes. People mostly want to escape the daily struggle of trying to make ends meet and to be comfortable. This is about trying to escape a state of 'constant worry' and becoming 'free from care'. Dole Animators participants drew themselves in the state that they felt they were in now and how they would like to imagine themselves. One woman depicted herself as someone with 'out of bed hair', 'clothes four years out of date' and 'scuffed Primark shoes'. She imagined how she might be if she was not struggling, with 'salon hair', 'nice clothes' and 'new shoes'.

Figure 3.2: Thrive's five-point plan to address poverty and insecurity

Source: Figure 3.2 was produced by participants at participatory workshops facilitated by Dan Farley and Ruth Patrick during 2016.

ATD Fourth World participants took a different approach. After detailed discussions, they decided that they would rather highlight one solution only, and build their image around this. The solution that felt most pertinent to them was the creation of a climate in which

Figure 3.3: Leeds-based Dole Animators' vision for a better, more secure future

Source: Figure 3.3 was produced by participants at participatory workshops facilitated by Dan Farley and Ruth Patrick during 2016.

the voices and expertise of those living in poverty are listened to, and better incorporated into public and political debate. In other words, the 'recognition', 'respect' and 'voice' which are commonly highlighted in the literature on poverty and social citizenship.[31]

Grassroots groups

The fourth participatory exercise consisted of nine two-hour sessions over a nine-month period with grassroots groups in the West Midlands. Organised by Michael Orton, each session had a facilitator and used interactive methods such as World Café, deliberative decision making, 'groan zone' and time for quiet reflection.

Sessions covered: first thoughts about content, criteria against which to judge ideas, identifying key themes, agreeing draft wording for each principle, reflecting on the process, consulting on emerging drafts, making revisions and agreeing examples of first steps. This exercise produced enormous amounts of data and identified more than 500 key words. This shows the complexity of the issues and illustrates the need for multivariate approaches to building a good society. At the same time, the complexity can paralyse action, and the volume of differing views means that it is hard to make progress. Given that the goal is simplicity, there need to be criteria for reducing the complexity to produce five principles. In whittling down the number of key actions, a voting procedure was used, as shown in Table 3.1.

Table 3.1: Criteria against which to judge ideas and actions

Criterion	'Votes'
Shifting the debate towards what you are 'for' not just 'against'	15
Fair and just society	14
Allow human flourishing	12
To inspire	11
Being positive, positive messages	9
Economic/ecological sustainability	9
Economy works better for everybody	8
Proper democracy	8
Social rather than individual	8
Unity and consistency	7
Helps inform how goals are achieved	7
Developing a new type of economy	5
Care-based economy	5
Clarify what's really important	5
To achieve equity	4
Be better heard	4
To get better politics	3
Help us stop squabbling among ourselves	2
Freedom and responsibility	2
Overcome isolation and disempowerment	2
Inclusive	2
Public utilities (transport) run for people not profit	1
Regulates markets	0
Combine principles and actions	0

Source: Table 3.1 was produced at participatory workshops for grassroots community groups in the West Midlands facilitated by Michael Orton

The groups finally agreed that the principles had to be positive, clear, concise, realistic, believable, tangible and durable, while being inclusive, motivating and inspiring so that they could act as a rallying point.

The principles to emerge were:

1. **Enabling potential:** Everyone has an equal opportunity to develop their full individual potential.
2. **Equal society:** Everyone is included and our basic human needs are provided for.
3. **Participatory democracy:** Everyone's voice is heard and every vote counts equally.
4. **Environmental sustainability:** Everyone feels our local environment is our home, and the planet is preserved for our children and grandchildren.
5. **An economy for the common good:** Everyone's needs are supported through regulated and responsible markets with mixed ownership models and by fostering local economies.

Drawing the threads together

Each of the four participatory research exercises developed a slightly different framework to summarise the results and any way of synthesising them involves compromise. However, this is an important point of principle from the participatory research: all the groups see compromise as a strength not a weakness. As the grassroots groups in the West Midlands concluded: "Building unity means being willing to listen, compromise and accept good enough outcomes."

That said, analysis of the work suggests almost total agreement on the importance of a good society that fulfils people's basic needs and enables them to feel safe. A good society means that people feel that they belong – that they are accepted, that relationships matter and that they are based on care, respect and fairness. A good society means that people take part in the decisions that affect them and have a voice in how things are run. A good society encourages creativity and fulfilment.

Michael Orton, who oversaw much of the participatory research described here and had access to the materials from the rest, drafted the five principles of a good society set out at the beginning of this chapter and road-tested them with various other groups. The criteria for selection were the same as those developed by the grassroots groups.

The five principles of a good society are not hard and fast; they are to be developed, modified and applied by people who want to take this forward.

This chapter shows that process is as important as product in constructing a good society. This is because such a society is not based on survey results or the theory of some dead economist or political scientist but is a lived experience constructed every day by society's members. Feelings matter and the acid test of a society is whether it is deemed good by the people who live in it. Engaging people over time and using creative methods to develop ideas enables complexity to emerge and compromises to be made so that competing views can be accommodated. Through this hard-won process, we can produce the society we want. How to do this? This is the question to be addressed in the next chapter.

Notes

[1]   Judt, T. (2010) *Ill fares the land*, London: Penguin Books, pp 1–2.

[2]   Berger, P.L. and Neuhaus, R.J. (1977) *To empower people: The role of mediating structures in public policy* (Vol 1), Washington, DC: AEI Press.

[3]   Bauman, Z. (2013) *Liquid modernity*, New York: John Wiley and Sons.

[4]   Lawson, N. (2009) *All consuming*, London: Penguin UK, p 52, p 10.

[5]   Debord, G. (1994) *The society of the spectacle*, New York, NY: Zone Books, p 17, p 42.

[6]   Davidson, B. (2016) The role of narrative change in influencing policy, 4 June. Available from: http://askjustice.org/2016/06/04/the-role-of-narrative-change-in-influencing-policy

[7]   Mattinson, B (2016) 'What do the public think of us and how can we speak in ways that understand each other?' Speech at Webb Memorial Trust, Oxfam and Shelter Workshop on Communications and Poverty, 29 January. Available from: www.webbmemorialtrust.org.uk/uncategorized/deborah-mattinson-britain-thinks-engaging-with-the-public-what-do-the-public-think-of-us-and-how-can-we-speak-in-ways-that-understand-each-other/

[8]   Lakoff, G. (2004) *Don't think of an elephant! Know your values and frame the debate – the essential guide for progressives*, Vermont: Chelsea Green Publishing.

[9]   Fritz, R. (1989) *The path of least resistance*, New York: Ballantine Books.

[10] Rogers, C. (1980) *A way of being*, New York: Mariner Books, p 240.

[11] Lederach, J.P. (2005) *The moral imagination: The art and soul of building peace*, New York: Oxford University Press.

[12] Lederach, J.P. (2005) p 73.

[13] Mills, C.W. (1959) *The sociological imagination*, New York, NY: Oxford University Press.

[14] Lederach, J.P. (2005) p 182.

[15] Hudson, L. (1967) *Contrary imaginations: A psychological study of the English schoolboy*, Harmondsworth: Penguin.

[16] Knight, B. (2015) *The society we want*, London: Alliance Publishing Trust and Webb Memorial Trust.

[17] Braudel, F. (1967) *A history of civilizations*, London: Penguin.

[18] Rosenmann, M. (2010) *Foundations for the common public good: Caring to change*. Available from: www.issuelab.org/resources/9341/9341.pdf

[19] Micklethwait, J. and Wooldridge, A. (2015) *The fourth revolution: The global race to reinvent the state*, London: Penguin.

[20] Mazower, M. (2009) *Dark continent: Europe's twentieth century*, London: Vintage.

[21] Lawson, N. (2016) *The context for a world without poverty*, Compass. Available from: www.compassonline.org.uk/publications/the-context-for-a-world-without-poverty

[22] Laing, R.D. (1973) *The divided self*, Harmondsworth: Penguin Books.

[23] Freud, A. (1992) *The ego and the mechanisms of defence*, London: Karnac Books.

[24] Laing, R.D. (1973) *The divided self*, Harmondsworth: Penguin Books, p 39.

[25] Knight, B., Chigudu, H. and Tandon, R. (2012) *Reviving democracy: Citizens at the heart of governance*, London: Routledge; Chambers, R. (1997) *Whose reality counts? Putting the first last*, London: Intermediate Technology Publications Ltd (ITP); Gaventa, J. (1982) *Power and powerlessness: Quiescence and rebellion in an Appalachian valley*, Champaign, IL: University of Illinois Press.

[26] Bennett, F. and Roberts, M. (2004) *From input to influence: Participatory approaches to research and inquiry into poverty*, York: Joseph Rowntree Foundation, p viii.

[27] Available from: www.children-ne.org.uk

[28] Young people around England (2014) *Poverty ends now*, Newcastle: Children North East and Webb Memorial Trust.

[29] Farthing, R. and Bryson, S. (2015) 'Poverty ends now', unpublished final report to the Webb Memorial Trust on a Children's antipoverty manifesto based on the work of 38 children.

[30] See www.brap.org.uk/the-name-game

[31] Lister, R. (2008) 'Recognition and voice: The challenge for social justice', in Craig, G., Burchardt, T. and Gordon, D. (eds) *Social justice and public policy: Seeking fairness in diverse societies*, Bristol: Policy Press.

FOUR

How do we achieve a good society without poverty?

This chapter begins by comparing the society we have with the society we want, and then considers how to close the gap. This brings us to our second framing question: 'How do we achieve a good society without poverty?'

This has been a central question for social reformers since Beatrice Webb's 1909 Minority Report challenged society to end destitution. Having considered some of the main methods to achieve this, the Trust research suggests that this is the wrong approach. The first question to ask is not 'how to do it?' but 'who does it?'

Comparing what we have and what we want

It is evident that the society we have (described in Chapter Two) is markedly different from the society we want (described in Chapter Three). Chapter Three suggested five principles of a good society:

1. We all have a decent basic standard of living.
2. So we are secure and free to choose how to lead our lives.

3. Developing our potential and flourishing materially and emotionally.
4. Participating, contributing and treating all with care and respect.
5. And building a fair and sustainable future for the next generations.

These five principles imply a society where people have sufficient wherewithal to be secure and free to live fulfilling lives. Achieving this would enable people to enjoy caring and respectful relationships and exercise their creativity, while helping to build sustainable futures for themselves and the coming generations.

The model of society we have now is based on the principle of individuals maximising their income. Success is measured by footfall in the shops and increases in per capita GDP each year. This approach has produced a society that helps a wealthy minority to flourish while one-fifth experience chronic poverty and many people on middle incomes fear for their futures.

What people want is security. Lying awake worrying about how to pay the bills is debilitating, causing stress that people carry over into their work and relationships. People want enough to pay their way and to have the occasional night out and holiday. While people desire modest prosperity, there is no evidence that they want to be rich or value a society where wealth is the emblem of success. Instead, the research suggests that the main yardstick for success is the quality of relationships they have.

What would a good society look like?

'Being able to leave the house without being afraid. Being able to earn a living not just earning enough money to survive.'

'An inclusive one in which everyone feels safe and secure.'

'A fair society where no one is exploited and everyone can live without fear and prejudice.'

'Everyone is secure and no one is at a disadvantage simply due to their race, sexuality or moral beliefs.'

'Security, safety, harmony, tolerance, support.'

'A sense of belonging, knowing how one fits in, feeling safe and being mutually supportive.'

Source: YouGov focus groups.

These findings are consistent with many findings from happiness research.[1] Once basic material wants have been satisfied, extra income adds very little to happiness. Economics appears as a supporting factor – essential up to a point to guarantee enough money to live a decent life. Beyond that, human relationships, social participation and human creativity become more important. These results echo the findings of psychologist Abraham Maslow, who developed a model of human personality in which economic factors are low down in our hierarchy of needs. Once these are satisfied, other needs – for belonging, recognition and self-actualisation – take over.[2] Philosopher Eric Fromm suggested that too much concern with 'having' impairs our 'being'. Liberation can be found in activities that move us towards solidarity and creativity. A concern with having leads us away from our true natures and alienates us from ourselves.[3] The quality of people's being in the world is more important than what they own.

The findings also echo the Buen Vivir movement in Latin America, which is based on the principles of harmony between human beings and nature leading to universal wellbeing.[4] The roots of the movement lie in indigenous traditions of balancing human needs with the environment. It is now being developed by activists and academics who are attempting to translate Buen Vivir into principles that can be adopted into the public sphere. There has been some success in Ecuador and Bolivia, where Buen Vivir has been adopted as part of the constitution. This is being translated into policy and practice through economies based on the principles of solidarity rather than growth.

The limits of economics

Economics appears to play a much less important part in our lives than politicians of all stripes would have us believe. And yet the economic paradigm is the dominant force in our world. Richard Easterlin concludes his 1996 defence of the unbridled free market, *Growth triumphant*, with the utopian vision of 'never ending economic growth, a world in which ever growing abundance is matched by ever rising aspirations, a world in which cultural differences are levelled in the constant race to achieve the good life of material plenty'.[5]

And yet, as the winner of the 2015 Webb Memorial Trust New Statesman Essay Prize, Beninio McDonough Tranza, put it:

> The quest of growth has left the economic and, increasingly the political power, of rich societies in the hands of unaccountable economic elites. It has intensified inequality between nations, condemning vast swathes of the world's population to ceaseless toil while others, less fortunate, beg for work to avoid starvation. Yet, most terrifyingly of all, it has led to the exploitation of the planet and its resources at such a scale that threatens the very existence of human civilization.[6]

So, while we should acknowledge that economic growth has brought benefits, there is much evidence that it has gone too far. The consequences can be seen in rising inequality, damage to the environment, and whole populations that have not benefited from the fruits of economic growth. Not only has it not succeeded in producing benefits for all; the prospect of wholesale collapse, which is never far from the surface in public debate, raises a bigger question about whether economics has failed more seriously. The inability to foresee the 2008 crash is cited by many as evidence of a serious problem at the heart of the discipline.[7]

There are attempts to reform economics from within. Billionaire philanthropist George Soros, for example, has set up the Institute for New Economic Thinking to find alternatives. Others, such as Robert and Edward Skidelsky, suggest that a society that gives precedence to economic growth and exalts material reward over all else is a poor society, downplaying what matters to people – leisure, knowledge, friendship and other goods that have no price.[8] They argue against Lionel Robbins' classic definition of economics as 'the science that studies human behaviour as a relationship between ends and scarce means which have alternative uses'.[9]

This puts scarcity at the centre of economics and excludes judgements of value; it effectively makes scarcity a permanent feature of the human condition. The book cites many counter-arguments to this view, originating from Aristotle's opinion that the practical business of making money is a means to an end, not an end. Keynes foresaw a future when economic growth combined with technological innovation would mean that work would be replaced by leisure as our main activity.[10] As Robert and Edward Skidelsky put it: 'Keynes lived most of his life in the nether regions of capitalist action, but he always had one eye on the heaven of art, love and the quest for knowledge.'[11]

The principle of scarcity means that society is always in deficit. The answer to scarcity is always 'more growth', yet scarcity always remains, demanding yet more growth. This, according to bestselling author Brené Brown, is a cause of much unhappiness. Her argument is that our sense of scarcity means 'We wake up in the morning and we say, "I didn't get enough sleep." And we hit the pillow saying, "I didn't get enough done."' She says that we're never thin enough, extraordinary enough or good enough – until we decide that we are. 'For me', she says, 'the opposite of scarcity is not abundance. It's *enough*. I'm enough. My kids are enough.'[12]

To get off this treadmill, we need to pursue something different. The five principles for a good society coming out of the study provide the kind of emotional sustenance that people want.

The research suggests that the preference given to economic rationalism over compassion is a serious error made by the political class. The next sections show that this error is compounded by the methods chosen to advance society. Although some of these methods have worked in the past, they no longer appear to do so. Following this, the beginnings of an approach that holds more promise will be set out.

The failure of top-down technocratic solutions

The traditional methods to produce social advance no longer work because they are driven by technocratic solutions rather than transformative processes. There are four main dimensions to this. First, the methods used are contested politically and are apt to be reversed by an incoming government, which means that the wellbeing of citizens is subject to a game of political ping-pong. Second, government programmes have been driven from the top down, based on unevaluated theories of change, rather than being developed using the skills, knowledge and expertise of people in communities. Third, the failure rate of public sector programmes has been high. Finally, the reliance on economic development, which once worked to lift people out of poverty, now fails to do so. Each of these points will be taken in turn.

Contested approaches

The question 'how do we end poverty?' divides people, which means there is always limited support for any approach. Although there is general agreement at all points on the political spectrum that reducing poverty is part of a good society, there is a split over methods between left and right, so policies are contested and likely to be reversed. The left believes that social and economic structure is the determining factor, while the right believes in individual agency. Those who favour structure see state solutions involving taxation and welfare as the means; those who favour agency see growth and jobs as the means. In neither case is there a clear pathway towards solving the issue.

Welfare reform – that is, reducing welfare benefits – sharply divides people. Those on the left mostly feel that the withdrawal of benefits will increase the proportion of people in poverty, while those on the right tend to suggest that people will find work and move out of poverty. In fact, as Mark Easton, home editor of the BBC, has pointed out, data so far offers no evidence as to whether welfare reform has a positive or a negative effect on poverty. Describing the release of official figures on poverty on 25 June 2015, he noted: 'The "experts" are scratching their heads. Today was the day, we were told, when we'd see a sharp rise in poverty as official figures included the full impact of welfare cuts for the first time.'

The evidence on 'Welfare to Work' programmes, invented by the Clinton administration in the US and adopted by Labour, Coalition and Conservative governments in the UK, is far from conclusive either way. In the US, there were expectations that poverty levels would rise as welfare benefits were withdrawn, but they did not; in fact they fell in the 1990s. At the same time, despite both Tony Blair and David Cameron publicly claiming that 'work is the best route out of poverty', the fastest growing category of people in poverty is the working poor.[13] The Joseph Rowntree Foundation concluded in December 2016 that 55 per cent of people in poverty are in working households. According to its *Monitoring poverty and social exclusion report*, the figures for the working poor are the highest ever.[14]

Attempts to find evidence for what works to reduce poverty are thin on the ground. The Joseph Rowntree Foundation commissioned a series of evidence reviews,[15] but these often rely on identifying risk factors associated with poverty, and there is no guarantee that reducing the risk factors will reduce poverty, because it would take very sophisticated multivariate analysis to unravel the effects of the different variables. The Trust put this to the test, commissioning the Smith Institute to identify the factors that led to improvements in poverty, and it was found that it was impossible to disentangle one factor from another. For this reason, a comprehensive and integrated strategy to end poverty is – methodologically speaking – a pipe dream. Paul Spicker has criticised the Joseph Rowntree Foundation strategy to end poverty because it is a collection of proposals that does not add up to a strategy.[16]

Top-down government programmes

For evidence of the drawbacks to top-down efforts to build a good society without poverty, there is no need to look further than the classic study of the 'War on Poverty' in 1960s America conducted by Peter Marris and Martin Rein.[17] In his efforts to create the 'Great Society', Lyndon B. Johnson founded the Office of Economic Opportunity to conduct a systematic programme to abolish poverty in America. Policies often failed to take root because powerful interest groups opposed the proposals, state officials were too hidebound to implement new ways of working, and labour unions resisted any change outside the immediate interests of their members.

Although less ambitious, Labour's flagship National Strategy for Neighbourhood Renewal also failed to gain traction. Launched in 2003, it aimed to end the persistence of large disparities between the most disadvantaged neighbourhoods and the rest of the country so that 'within 10 to 20 years, no-one should be seriously disadvantaged by where they live'. Acknowledging that previous regeneration programmes had failed to reverse neighbourhood decline, the strategy aimed to tackle the causes of deprivation comprehensively, focusing on the poorest neighbourhoods in the country and considering the interrelationships between those causes of deprivation. Its goals were to improve education and skills, health and housing, while reducing worklessness and crime. The programme was ended early by the Treasury because of lack of progress. Although evaluations show that there were some positive results,[18] there were few signs of the wholesale transformation intended.[19]

Such an observation could be made of government regeneration schemes over many decades. In a review of area-based regeneration conducted for the Trust, Steve Osborn noted:

> The lessons from more than 40 or so years of neighbourhood regeneration schemes, since the Urban Programme in the late 1960s, are not encouraging. Although there have been some successful schemes, and there is no doubt that some

neighbourhoods have been physically transformed, the general picture is of disadvantaged neighbourhoods remaining disadvantaged despite repeated interventions.[20]

While there have been some examples of success, such as the major housebuilding programme after the Second World War, the overall findings from evaluation of regeneration programmes have been gloomy. To take a specific example, a workshop held to review developments in Benwell, an area of multiple disadvantage in the West End of Newcastle, concluded that, beginning in the late 1960s with the National Community Development Project, the area had become a 'laboratory for government policies' and yet remained one of the poorest of the country.[21] The workshop concluded with a reflection on the many times that local people had been consulted as part of strategic planning: 'history shows us that the Benwell community is very good at "imagining" better futures. But we have also to keep asking why so often they cannot have what they ask for.' Examination of the distribution of poverty across the country shows us that the Webbs' 'cities of poverty' are still with us.[22]

High failure rate of public sector programmes

The evidence suggests that public intervention does not guarantee success. Public spending does not necessarily lead to positive outcomes because the money is easily absorbed by the system without productive output. There are many failed government programmes, described by Crewe and King's *The blunders of our governments*,[23] the latest well-meaning failure being the Troubled Families Initiative.[24]

In *Seeing like a state*, James Scott catalogues the failures caused by state planners applying so-called scientific blueprints without incorporating the know-how of local communities into planning processes.[25] Technology writer Evgeny Morozov has labelled this approach 'solutionism', and suggests it limits our ability to think creatively about the nature of the problems we want to solve.[26] In its extreme form, solutionism leads to precise numerical targets to measure social advance. But, as Tim Harford has shown, targets are no guarantee of solving the problem because it is easy to 'hit the target, but miss the point'.[27]

One reason why state solutions have failed to gain traction is that it has become progressively more difficult to use 'social administration' solutions to reduce poverty. The 1944 Bretton Woods arrangements enabled states to run their own economies insulated from the shocks of international markets. But these arrangements were abandoned in 1971. From that time, states have not had the means to ensure the welfare of all their citizens, even in a society that is generally more wealthy. Despite many years of efforts to reduce poverty in a rising economy, the bottom quintile has living standards way below what is expected in a modern country.

This was the quandary the Trust tried to unravel when it supported a Fabian Society project called 'Poverty in the age of affluence' in 2006. It is noteworthy that in the final publication of the Fabian Society project, *The solidarity society* (2009),[28] proposals to end poverty relied almost entirely on central government action through increased public expenditure. By the time of its publication, it was clear that the 2008 crash had cut the ground from under such proposals. The public sector would have fewer resources and reduced capacity to deliver.

Growth fails to deliver

According to *The Economist*, economic development has taken almost a billion people out of poverty in the past 20 years.[29] Michelthwait and Wooldridge, in their influential book *The fourth revolution*, suggest that economic growth is the only sustainable way to reduce poverty in the future.[30]

The Trust research suggests that, its achievements globally notwithstanding, economic growth fails as a solution in the UK for several reasons. The Trust commissioned Neil McInroy of the Centre for Local Economic Strategies to examine the processes of economic development. He reviewed the literature, including the work of Nobel Laureate Simon Kuznets, who suggests that inequality and disadvantage decrease as an economy develops. This is the theory of 'trickle-down', which suggests that once private investment capital is secured, economic and social success will follow as supply chain benefits and local jobs are created. McInroy shows that such an approach does not work, and that economic growth fails to lift those at the bottom much beyond subsistence level. Yet the view that economic growth will bring prosperity for all has been a key plank of government policy since the war. McInroy calls this 'boomgoggling' – the tendency to see economic boom and social benefit as inevitable. He describes this as 'an optimism bias which goes unrecognised'.[31]

One of the main reasons for the failure of trickle-down is the way in which the market distributes its rewards – a process called 'predistribution'. In the US, Jacob Hacker and Paul Pierson found that policies governing financial markets, the rights of unions and the pay of top executives have all shifted in favour of those at the top, especially the financial and non-financial executives who make up about six in ten of the richest 0.1 per cent of Americans.[32] This work inspired the Trust's support for the Smith Institute study on workplace democracy, *Just deserts*, which suggested a greater role for employees in making decisions at work,[33] and a High Pay Commission study on the business case for moderating executive remuneration.[34] The rewards of economic growth do not benefit most people. In fact wage rates have not risen. Although employment rates were at an all-time high in November 2016,[35] long-term economic trends have removed well-paying jobs from the economy, so that the fastest growing category of people in poverty has been those in work.[36] Tracy Shildrick and colleagues coined the expression 'low pay no pay cycle' to describe the experience of many people as they move in and out of badly paid work.[37]

Prospects for the future of work are dim. As technology continues to replace people with machines, the likelihood of well-paying work for the mass of the population is diminishing. Research in 2013 by two Oxford economists, Frey and Osborne, concludes that, in the next two decades, 47 per cent of employment will be 'in the high-risk category', meaning that it is 'potentially automatable'. It is mainly less well-paid workers who are most at risk.[38] Consequently, there is a move towards what the OECD calls 'inclusive growth',[39] in which the benefits of economic growth are shared more widely. The Royal Society of Arts has set up a City Growth Commission to examine the challenges to cities posed by demographic shifts, climate change, pressures on public finances and economic uncertainty.[40] It is too soon to say whether this new approach will address the deep problems that we now face.

System failure

The surest sign that the twin pillars of the postwar settlement – social security and economic development – are no longer sufficient to reduce poverty is the fact that, in some cases, social security now subsidises the private sector rather than poor people. Take, for example, tax credits. Introduced in 1999 and developed through the Tax Credits Act 2002, their main purpose is to help families on lower pay make ends meet. They are also intended to lift families out of welfare dependency and provide incentives for people to work. As Peter Kenway has pointed out, the cost has been large and 'displaces the older idea, which underpinned the original design of the Welfare State, that the role of a social security system is to provide an adequate income in the event that a household lacks work'.[41] Rather than providing sustainable solutions to poverty, critics have suggested that the social security system subsidises the private sector. Citizens UK calculates that the Treasury pays out £11 billion a year in benefits and tax credits to the 22 per cent of the UK workforce who are paid less than the living wage. Five firms alone (Tesco, Asda, Sainsbury's, Morrison's and Next) are subsidised to the tune of £1 billion a year – despite making a profit in the UK.[42]

A second example of social security subsidising the private sector is housing benefit, where money is paid to private landlords charging high rents rather than building and sustaining low-cost housing.[43] Such a use of the social security system is a sure sign that it has lost its way.

Need for a rethink in face of a 'trilemma'

The long-term failure of state action and private enterprise, which brought gains in society during the 'thirty glorious years' from 1945, is no longer fit for purpose. At the heart of the problem is what Toby Lloyd, head of policy at Shelter, calls a 'trilemma':

> By this I mean that it is impossible to simultaneously avoid widespread destitution; an ever-rising welfare bill; and major state intervention into key markets. It should be possible to avoid one or even two of these at once – but not all three. At any given point in history society is effectively making a choice to embrace, or at least tolerate, one of these three options. It may not be explicit, but by prioritising the avoidance of one or two of these outcomes, we are implicitly agreeing to put up with the third as the lesser of three evils.[44]

If we continue to use our current framing, it is hard to see how we can find a way through this. First, the market no longer produces good jobs for people. A report the Trust commissioned from CPAG and Working Families demonstrates fundamental changes in the organisation of the economy which mean that low-paid work is likely to become more prevalent. Second, increasing welfare payments does little to address the underlying causes of poverty and is unsustainable: as a strategy it is politically unpopular and runs counter to the idea of a society of empowered individuals who are in control of their lives. Third, the scope for state intervention in markets is limited if it involves significant expenditure. Given that the size of the public debt reached an all-time high in December 2016,[45] there is no reserve to fund development without an increase in taxes. Even if there were, there is no clear pathway for the state to follow to reduce poverty. As we have seen, state initiatives have often failed.

Put this way, we cannot make progress if we frame poverty as a problem to be solved. This is because such framing places poverty as an undesirable by-product of the society we want. As *Big Issue* founder

John Bird has pointed out, as consumers, we want cheap goods. We therefore commit ourselves to low pay to keep our costs down, and so create poverty and tolerate it as 'collateral damage wrought by an otherwise buoyant marketplace'.[46] In other words, if our societal goal is a thriving capitalist society then we must accept poverty as part of that. As Bird puts it, poverty is 'the backbone of contemporary capitalism'. This chimes with the work of Zygmunt Bauman, who suggests that poverty is embedded in the system because the poor are useful. In a society based on production of goods, the poor are useful as a pool of cheap labour. In a consumer society, he suggests, their main role is to be humiliated as a warning to the rest of us not to fall off the consumer treadmill and become one of the undeserving poor. [47]

The conclusion from the Trust's research is that a complete rethink is necessary. Although economic development, improved welfare policies and state intervention once lifted our society, they are not fit for purpose for the future. Results of a consultation commissioned from Compass confirmed that the days of tweaking a failing system are over: what is needed is reform of the whole system. At the heart of this is a change in values that establishes the end of poverty as a necessity for the future of our society – one of several features of a good society rather than something to be repaired as 'collateral damage of a buoyant marketplace'. In this way, poverty reduction would become an integral feature of a good society rather than a compensatory afterthought.

Why a complete rethink is necessary
Situation

'Brexit as a rational decision of the voiceless and the humiliated.'

'Alienated working class.'

'The supply side won't deliver a good society; we need new and inclusive policies.'

'A lack of coherent agency.'

'Referendum showed people use power when they have it.'

Possibilities

'Can we put jump leads on dinosaurs (the political parties)?'

'Go local, to listen and to connect.'

'Communities need to find solutions not have them imposed.'

'Develop new political spaces that are fun, accessible; start where people are.'

Source: Compass consultation, held the weekend after the referendum on the future of the EU.

This approach involves radical change. We cannot solve poverty through a series of technocratic fixes that treat society as if it were a machine. Instead, we need transformational processes that regard society as an ecosystem where everyone is included in developing the society we want. If a good society is to be achieved, it must be achieved organically within society. Society's elites can and must help to do this but they cannot lay down blueprints.

The great error of the delivery of the welfare state was the principle that 'the gentleman in Whitehall knows best'. The postwar settlement enabled people to be passive in relation to questions of employment and social security. In 'Why successful movements are all about relationships', Hilary Cottam describes 'Beveridge's mistake' on the welfare state:[48] people were 'done to', not 'done with'. Similarly, Julien Le Grand's famous 1997 study 'Knights and knaves' characterises the public as 'pawns'.[49] Towards the end of his life, Beveridge saw that the welfare state undermined what people acting together could do to bring social advance and argued for the government to promote a vigorous programme of mutual aid.[50] However, the damage was done because – initially – the system was good at providing jobs, services and benefits. As seen in Chapter One, when the defects of the system became clear, the cold bureaucracy of the state began to be hated by people who depended on it.

In post-Brexit Britain, where contempt for the establishment is widespread, ordinary people, particularly young people, are no longer willing to play a passive role and accept blueprints handed down from above. The growth of Poverty Truth Commissions, and their slogan of 'Nothing about us without us is for us', is emblematic of the new mood. An example of what people can do for themselves is the Living Wage Campaign. Ordinary people in the East End of London – despite their evident diversity – united around a common aim and changed government policy from below. If enough people want change, change will happen.

These examples show that ordinary people, including those on low incomes, are competent to run their own affairs. This exposes what historian E.P. Thompson described as two fallacies.[51] One is what he called the 'Fabian orthodoxy', in which 'the great majority of working people are seen as passive victims of laissez faire'. The other is the 'orthodoxy of the empirical economic historians', in which working people are seen as 'a labour force, as migrants, or as the data for statistical series'. We must recognise that people have power and agency. This, as John Bird shows, through both his work and his writings, includes people who are poor.[52]

Who not how

So, the question 'how do we end poverty?' is the wrong one. The question should not be how do we develop a good society without poverty, but who should do it? Answers to this question imply responsibility, agency and power.

One of the chief merits of the 'who question' is that it avoids the polarisation of the current debate, based on the dichotomy of government versus individual responsibility. From the point of view of the social science literature, agency and structure are two sides of the same coin of social change. Agency – the capacity of individuals to act independently and to make their own choices – takes place in the context of structure. Structure is the amalgam of factors of influence (such as social class, religion, gender, ethnicity and customs) that determine or limit an agent and his or her decisions.[53] The relative influence of structure and agency is unclear. The evidence gives us no reason to say that one dominates the other.[54] The main point is that both agency and structure matter. We need to find common ground while embracing a multiplicity of views about what is good for progress. We need to be inclusive and to find accommodations between different views. As the survey responses show, idealists (who favour structural solutions) and libertarians (who favour individual solutions) are both in a minority.

On this view, poverty is a 'systemic' issue, rather than merely structural or individual. The solution depends on all parts of the system. Everyone has a role to play, as suggested in the *New Statesman* in November 2015, where interim results of the Trust's research were published:

> Who should solve the problem of poverty? This is a central question posed by the Webb Memorial Trust in its latest research to define a good society. Our answer is 'everyone'.[55]

Arising from this, if everyone has responsibility for poverty, how does each of the parties fulfil its responsibilities? A crucial precondition of everyone being involved is ownership. Connell and Kubisch argue that the success of any initiative depends on the people who make change happen being involved at the outset.[56] Making recommendations at the end of a process that has not involved key agencies is unlikely to work because the agencies have no ownership of the results.

Looked at in this way, society becomes a self-organising system in which everyone is tasked with helping to create the economy and society we want. The key is relationships. One of the reasons why Citizens UK has been so successful is that its approach puts citizens' relationships with one another at the heart of its work. In her contribution to the 2014 Webb Memorial Trust *New Statesman Poverty Supplement*, Ruth Lister stresses the importance of participation in reaching societal solutions and cites the Commission on Poverty, Participation and Power as an example of good practice, with half of its members having had direct experience of poverty.[57]

Participation plays a vital part in developing society.[58] There is a line of history, almost entirely disregarded by current thinkers, that traces connections between John Ruskin's *Unto this last*, first published as essays in 1860, its translation into Gujarat by Gandhi in 1908, and its influence on the campaign for Indian independence, and subsequently on the civil rights movement in the US and the broad-based organising of Citizens UK. The central point is that transformative power is found in relationships that are shared and not hoarded.

Towards a new paradigm built on compromise

Participation offers an alternative to the prevailing view of society, one that values non-material qualities as well as material ones. As the research suggests, there is an impressive consistency in what most people want – security, fairness and independence. The narrative is dominated by social factors rather than economic ones.

To find this new paradigm will require compromise: the old bifurcation between right and left leads us to nowhere but conflict. While there are substantive differences of view between people and vested interests on the left and right that will resist change, which guarantee that the road to compromise is fraught with difficulty, the research suggests that this is the only route that will deliver the society most ordinary people want. At the outset of the research programme two trustees of the Webb Memorial Trust, who happened to be members of parliament, Kate Green (Labour) and Chris White (Conservative), wrote a joint article in the *New Statesman* in which they pointed out that 'no political party "owns" the issue of poverty, and that all parties have an interest in working together to create long-term consensus around policies'.[59] They further suggested that:

if we are going to create a broader consensus on tackling poverty, politicians need to ensure that they work not just between themselves but also with interest groups, charities and businesses. Given the important role that these organisations play in feeding into the political process, and the way in which their practices too will impact directly on individuals' experience of poverty, any effort to improve communications and develop solutions on poverty must also include these important players.

Following this article, the Trust supported the All Party Parliamentary Group on Poverty and this has become an important vehicle for dissemination of its work and discussion of other questions related to poverty across the parties. The Trust was encouraged in this direction by Paul Addison's observation in *The road to 1945* that the postwar consensus emerged during the Second World War because of cross-party discussions. An important suggestion was made by a Conservative, Quintin Hogg, that social security for all needed to be the leitmotif of the peace.[60]

The idea of security seems to be the foundation stone of a good society in the minds of most ordinary people, and it is an idea that has resonance across all the main political parties. For this reason, the concept is a good starting point for building compromise. The Trust therefore decided to use the term 'security' not 'poverty' as a way of introducing discussions about a good society without poverty. To take this further, Michael Orton was asked to develop ideas from across the political spectrum and to explore with various actors in politics, academia, think tanks and civil society the potential for ideas to build a consensus. Unlike much social research, this did not lean towards the left or the right. It drew on work from a wide range of political traditions. Thus, the right-leaning Centre for Social Justice, Civitas, Bright Blue and The Good Right were cited alongside left-leaning organisations such as the Fabian Society and Friends of the Earth. The *Daily Telegraph*'s James Kirkup was quoted, as was *The Guardian*'s Polly Toynbee. As Michael Orton points out:

The fetishising of the state, markets, family and so on is avoided and, instead, recognition is given to a role for the public and private, the collective and the individual, the financial and the relational, the state and civil society and communities and families.[61]

The results of the research were launched at an All Party Parliamentary Group on Poverty meeting in 2016 as *Secure and free*.[62] The report identifies what Orton calls '5+ ideas'. These are five substantive suggestions to foster social and economic security, together with some add-ons. The ideas, together with their sources, are expressed by Michael Orton as follows:

1. 'Above inflation increases [in the national minimum wage level] should become the norm in periods of economic growth until there is an indication of a negative impact on employment' (Centre for Social Justice) + 'Make improving productivity and improving the quality of employment mutually reinforcing policy objectives' (Smith Institute).
2. 'A Harold Macmillan-sized, state-supported housebuilding programme ... designed to the highest environmental standards' (The Good Right) + Improve 'security for home-owners through ... a "right to sell" and a "right to stay", so that those who can no longer meet mortgage repayments can sell their properties but remain as tenants paying fair rents' (Friends of the Earth) + 'Curb future rent growth and improve security for tenants' (Civitas).
3. 'Unleash the power of the social sector' (Centre for Social Justice) + Implement non-financial help for families and relationship support (various).
4. Make early childhood education and care a specific and distinct element of the universal care and education system, free at the point of delivery (various) + 'Significant real increases to child benefit' (Fabian Society and Sir Tony Atkinson).
5. Given the current lack of consensus about how to provide a decent basic standard of living, Compass offers to work with other civil

society groups on building agreement around a shift from welfare for some to social security for all right through to older age + many social actors from across the political spectrum commented that democratic renewal is a necessary condition for change – so relevant additional ideas are put forward.

These ideas have been well received and could form a good starting point for building a consensus about a good society. Chapter Five looks at how this might be done and the roles different groups might play.

Notes

[1] Layard, R. (2011) *Happiness: Lessons from a new science*, London: Penguin UK.

[2] Maslow, A.H. (1943) 'A theory of human motivation', *Psychological review*, 50(4): 370.

[3] Fromm, E. (1978) *To have or to be?*, London: Jonathan Cape.

[4] Heinrich Böhl Stiftung (2011) 'Buen Vivir: Latin America's new concepts for the good life and the rights of nature'. Available from: www.boell.de/en/content/buen-vivir-latin-americas-new-concepts-good-life-and-rights-nature; Balch, O. (2013) 'Buen vivir: The social philosophy inspiring movements in South America', *The Guardian*, 4 February.

[5] Easterlin, R.A. (1996) *Growth triumphant*, Ann Arbor: Michigan University Press, p 156.

[6] Tranza, B.M. (2016) 'How can growth reduce equality?', *New Statesman*, 10 February.

[7] Chu, B. (2014) 'Manchester students man the barricades to overthrow economic orthodoxy', *The Independent*, 25 April.

[8] Skidelsky, R. and Skidelsky, E. (2013) *How much is enough: The love of money and the case for the good life*, London: Allen Lane.

[9] Robbins, L. (1935) *An Essay on the nature and significance of economic science*. Revised edition, London: MacMillan, p 36.

[10] Keynes, J.M. (1930) 'Economic possibilities for our grandchildren', *The Nation and Athenaeum*, 48(3): 358–373.

[11] Skidelsky, R. and Skidelsky, E. (2013) *How much is enough: The love of money and the case for the good life*, London: Allen Lane, p 37.

[12] Flintoff, J. (2013) 'Brené Brown: "People are sick of being afraid all the time"', *The Guardian*, 27 July.

[13] Easton, M. (2015) 'Is welfare reform working?', BBC, 25 June 2015. Available from: www.bbc.co.uk/news/uk-33275936

[14] Joseph Rowntree Foundation (2016) *Monitoring poverty and social exclusion 2016*, York: Joseph Rowntree Foundation.

[15] Joseph Rowntree Foundation (2014) *Reducing poverty in the UK: A collection of evidence reviews.* Available from: www.jrf.org.uk/sites/default/files/jrf/migrated/files/Reducing-poverty-reviews-FULL_0.pdf

[16] Spicker, P. (2016) 'The Joseph Rowntree Foundation thinks it can solve poverty. It won't do it this way', 9 September. Available from: http://blog.spicker.uk/the-joseph-rowntree-foundation-thinks-it-can-solve-poverty-it-wont-do-it-this-way

[17] Marris, P. and Rein, M. (1972) *Dilemmas of social reform*, Harmondsworth: Penguin.

[18] Lupton, R., Fenton, A. and Fitzgerald, A. (2013) 'Labour's record on neighbourhood renewal in England: Policy, spending and outcomes 1997–2010', *Social policy in a cold climate*, Working Paper 6, CASE, London School of Economics .

[19] Crisp, R., Pearson, S. and Gore, T. (2015) 'Rethinking the impact of regeneration on poverty: A (partial) defence of a "failed" policy', *Journal of Poverty and Social Justice*, 23(3): 167–187. Available from: http://dx.doi.org/10.1332/175982715X14443317211905

[20] Osborn, S. (2011) 'People, places and poverty: getting away from the neighbourhood', in Knight, B. (ed) *A minority view: What Beatrice Webb would say now*, London: Alliance Publishing Trust and Webb Memorial Trust, p 71.

[21] Armstrong, A., Banks, S. and Harman, P. (2016) 'Imagining Benwell workshop and exhibtion', 21 January. Available from: www.imaginenortheast.org/wp-content/uploads/2016/02/Imagining-Benwell-Workshop-Report-21.1.16-final-version.pdf

[22] End Child Poverty publishes new figures on the level of child poverty in each constituency, local authority and ward in the UK. Available from: www.endchildpoverty.org.uk/poverty-in-your-area-2016

[23] Crewe, I. and King, A. (2013) *The blunders of our governments*, London: Oneworld.

[24] Day, L., Bryson, C., White, C., Purdon, S., Bewley, H., Kirchner Sala, L. and Portes, J. (2016) *National evaluation of the Troubled Families Programme*, October, London: Department for Communities and Local Government.

[25] Scott, J.C. (1998) *Seeing like a state: How certain schemes to improve the human condition have failed*, Princeton, NJ: Princeton University Press.

[26] Morozov, E. (2013) *To save everything, click here: The folly of technological solutionism*, London: Allen Lane.

[27] Harford, T. (2016) *Messy: How to be creative and resilient in a tidy minded world*, London: Little Brown, p 170.

[28] Horton, T. and Gregory, J. (2009) *The solidarity society: Fighting poverty in an age of affluence 1909–2009*, London: Fabian Society and Webb Memorial Trust.

[29] *The Economist* (2013) 'Towards the end of poverty', 1 June.

[30] Micklethwait, J. and Wooldridge, A. (2015) *The fourth revolution: The global race to reinvent the state*, London: Penguin.

[31] McInroy, N. (2016) *Forging a good local society: Tackling poverty through a local economic reset*, Manchester: Centre for Local Economic Strategies and Webb Memorial Trust, p 11.

[32] Hacker, J.S. and Pierson, P. (2010) *Winner takes all politics: How Washington made the rich richer – and turned its back on the middle class*, New York: Simon and Schuster.

[33] Coates, D. (2013) *Just deserts: Poverty and income inequality: Can workplace democracy make a difference?*, London: Smith Institute and Webb Memorial Trust.

[34] The High Pay Centre (2014) *The High Cost of High Pay*, London: High Pay Centre.

[35] Source: Trading Economics. Available from: www.tradingeconomics.com/united-kingdom/unemployment-rate

[36] Schuemecher, K. (2014) *Future of the UK labour market*, York: Joseph Rowntree Foundation. Available from: www.jrf.org.uk/sites/default/files/jrf/files-research/poverty-jobs-worklessness-summary.pdf

[37] Shildrick, T., MacDonald, R. and Garthwaite, K. (2010) *The low-pay, no-pay cycle: Understanding recurrent poverty*, York: Joseph Rowntree Foundation. Available from: www.jrf.org.uk/report/low-pay-no-pay-cycle-understanding-recurrent-poverty

[38] Frey, C.B. and Osborne, M. (2013) *The future of employment: How susceptible are jobs to computerisation?*, Oxford: Martin School.

[39] OECD (2015) *All on board: Making inclusive growth happen*. Available from: www.keepeek.com/Digital-Asset-Management/oecd/development/all-on-board/executive-summary_9789264218512-2-en#.WlrsdDtC5dg#page2

[40] See the City Growth Commission. Available from: www.thersa.org/action-and-research/rsa-projects/public-services-and-communities-folder/city-growth-commission

[41] Kenway, P. (2011) 'Low income households should not be taxed until they can afford it', in Knight, B. (ed) *A minority view: What Beatrice Webb would say now*, Alliance Publishing Trust and Webb Memorial Trust, p 52.

[42] Waugh R. (2015) 'Supermarkets pay workers so little the government has to chip in £11bn a year', *Metro*, 13 April.

[43] Webb, K. (2012) *Bricks or benefits? Rebalancing housing investment*, London: Shelter.

[44] Lloyd, T. (2017) '"Intervention needed" to reduce welfare bill without causing more poverty', in Webb Memorial Trust, *Housing, poverty and the good society: What can we achieve by 2025?* Available from: www.webbmemorialtrust.org.uk/home-page/housing-poverty-and-the-good-society-what-can-we-achieve-by-2025

[45] Khan, M. (2016) 'UK public sector net debt hits highest on record at £1.65tn', *Financial Times*, 21 December.

[46] Bird, J. (2012) 'Poverty is not a failure of capitalism, but its backbone', Ceasefire Magazine, 27 November. Available from: https://ceasefiremagazine.co.uk/john-bird-poverty-failure-capitalism-backbone/

[47] Bauman, Z. (1998) *Work, consumerism and the new poor*, Milton Keynes: Open University Press.

[48] Cottam, H. (2014) 'Why successful movements are all about relationships', *New Statesman*, 2 May.

[49] Le Grand, J. (1997) 'Knights, knaves or pawns? Human behaviour and social policy', *Journal of Social Policy*, 26(2): 149–69.

[50] Beveridge, W. (1948) *Voluntary action*, London: George Allen and Unwin.

[51] Thompson, E.P. (1963) *The making of the English working class*, London: Victor Gollancz, p 2.

[52] Bird, J. (2012) *The necessity of poverty*, London: Quartet Books.

[53] Barker, C. (2005) *Cultural studies: Theory and practice*, London: Sage.

[54] Littlejohn, S.W. and Foss, K.A. (2009). 'Agency', in Littlejohn, S.W. and Foss, K.A. (eds) *Encyclopedia of communication theory*, Thousand Oaks, CA: SAGE Publications Inc.

[55] Knight, B. (2015) 'Positive action in the workplace', Webb Memorial Trust Supplement, *New Statesman*, 23 October, p 3.

[56] Connell, J.P. and Kubisch, A.C. (1998) 'Applying a theory of change approach', in Fulbright Anderson, K., Kubisch, A.C. and Connell, J.P. (eds) *New approaches to evaluating community initiatives volume 2: Theory, measurement, and analysis*, Washington, DC: The Aspen Institute.

[57] Lister, R. (2014) 'Creating participatory inclusive engagement', *New Statesman*, 2 May.

[58] Thompson, E.P. (1963) *The making of the English working class*, London: Victor Gollancz.

[59] Green, K. and White, C. (2012) 'Altogether better', *New Statesman*, 27 February.

[60] Addison, P. (1975) *The road to 1945: British politics and the Second World War*, London: Jonathan Cape.

[61] Orton, M. (2016) 'Tackling insecurity. Here's a plan published from the Left but with solutions for the Right – and for everyone else', 6 May. Available from: www.conservativehome.com/platform/2016/05/michael-orton-tackling-insecurity-heres-a-plan-published-from-the-left-but-with-solutions-for-the-right-and-for-everyone-else.html

[62] Orton, M. (2016) *Secure and free: 5+ solutions to socio-economic insecurity*, London: Compass.

FIVE

Who does what to produce a good society?

Chapter Three suggested that the key to producing a good society without poverty is the pursuit of five principles through a process in which everyone is involved. To recap, these principles are:

1. We all have a decent basic standard of living.
2. So we are secure and free to choose how to lead our lives.
3. Developing our potential and flourishing materially and emotionally.
4. Participating, contributing and treating all with care and respect.
5. And building a fair and sustainable future for the next generations.

This chapter considers the question of 'who does what?' to achieve these principles. While it cannot prescribe what people do, various pointers are suggested emerging from the research that will take things forward and develop a better balance in our society over the long term.

Who will take responsibility?

Chapter Three found that asking people how to reduce poverty tends to divide them along the lines of social structure versus personal agency.

Asking 'who is responsible?' is more promising. One of the questions asked in the population research with YouGov was: 'Thinking about reducing poverty, how much, if any, responsibility do you think each of the following groups should have to achieve this?' Answer options included: 'a great deal of responsibility', 'a fair amount of responsibility', 'not a lot of responsibility', 'no responsibility at all' and 'don't know'. The proportion of the 10,112 adults who answered 'a great deal' is shown in Figure 5.1.

Clearly, respondents felt that many agencies have a role to play in reducing poverty. In fact, they would typically see a configuration of agencies playing a part. Poverty, it would seem, is everyone's business.

How might this work in concrete terms? This section draws on the work that Michael Orton conducted for the Trust on consensus building. He points out that employers could pay the living wage, invest in training and facilitate progression for staff. Government could and does control benefit levels, taxation and legislation in a wide range of relevant fields. Philanthropists could spend their money tackling poverty. Local action could and does build relationships between people. However, not all of us are motivated by a desire to reduce poverty. The risk is that, while we all acknowledge our responsibility, we simply pay lip service to it. As Orton points out, it is important to identify the agents.[1]

As seen in Chapter One, the poverty lobby sees the government as the main agent of change, and this explains the common pattern where think tanks say that 'the results demonstrate a challenge to government'. Yet, as previous chapters have demonstrated, government itself is commonly at a loss what to do. A corollary of the way the 'who?' question is being answered is that everyone who wants to see change takes responsibility for making it happen, rather than preaching to others to do so.

From what basis should we work? This book has suggested five principles for a good society that, while not comprehensive, prevent the pitfalls of starting from scratch, working within the confines of narrow organisational goals producing policy shopping lists or yet another individual manifesto. These five principles are a useful starting

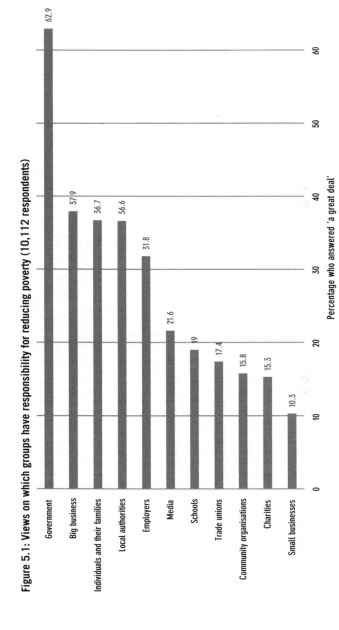

Figure 5.1: Views on which groups have responsibility for reducing poverty (10,112 respondents)

Government — 62.9
Big business — 37.9
Individuals and their families — 36.7
Local authorities — 36.6
Employers — 31.8
Media — 21.6
Schools — 19
Trade unions — 17.4
Community organisations — 15.8
Charities — 15.3
Small businesses — 10.3

Percentage who answered 'a great deal'

Source: YouGov Survey of 10,112 adults from England, Scotland and Wales in January 2015

point to build consensus. Consensus does not imply full agreement. The 'tyranny of perfection', which means that everyone must agree with every word, is a considerable handicap in producing something of value. The need for compromise has emerged as a core principle in the Trust's work, and could be said to be the foundation of a democratic society.

However, there should be broad agreement on principles. In developing and implementing the philosophy of neoliberalism, the 450 US think tanks that developed the five core messages (free markets, small state, low tax, individual liberty and big defence) campaigned with a shared vision on these general principles rather than detailed policy objectives and methods.

One of the first steps should be cooperation rather than competition between those involved in combating poverty. As Orton notes: 'instead of working together, poverty is a contest between competing ideas, arguments and interests, something that is fought over, albeit in non-violent ways'.[2] For example, in the space of one week in September 2016 three leading organisations launched separate reports on poverty and inequality without reference to each other. Behind this is the larger problem that the 160,000 organisations that share overlapping values such as equality, democracy and social justice have no coherence; their messages are splintered in thousands of reports and millions of tweets without making serious progress as a clear force for change. A critical question is 'how do we join up the efforts of different groups and people who desire the principles behind the society we want?'

How do we create change?

How do we create change? As Paul Mason puts it in *Postcapitalism*:

> If you believe that there is a better system than capitalism, then the past twenty-five years have felt like being – as Alexander Bognadov put it – 'a Martian stranded on Earth'. You have a clear view of what society should be like, but no means of getting there.[3]

What drives change, suggests Mason, is the network – a group of interrelated individuals and organisations that can see better futures and act together in loose affiliation. This is an important view and one supported by history. Arnold Toynbee suggests that civilisations develop in different ways because of their different environments and different approaches to the challenges they face. Critical to development are 'creative minorities'.[4] These are the people who find solutions to the challenges, which others then follow. In an earlier generation, Samuel Taylor Coleridge stressed the importance of what he termed the 'clerisy' in society.[5] Today, we might call this group 'thought leaders' or 'intelligentsia'. Their importance is that they recognise the best in the national cultural heritage and raise the standard of intellectual life. In doing this, they enable society to remain stable while making progress.

At various times in the past, networks have been responsible for creating societal change. Take, for example, the Bloomsbury Group. This was an influential group of English writers, intellectuals, philosophers and artists who lived, worked and studied together near Bloomsbury, London, during the first half of the 20th century. This loose collective of friends and relatives included Virginia Woolf, John Maynard Keynes, E.M. Forster and Lytton Strachey. Their works and outlook deeply influenced literature, aesthetics, criticism and economics as well as modern attitudes towards feminism, pacifism and sexuality. Similarly, the group around the Webbs was highly influential in developing the platform for the coming of the welfare state.

We need a group like this to emerge out of the mass of civil society to move society on to a more progressive platform based on the five principles set out in Chapter Three. Central to how a small network makes progress are two vital ideas: creativity and leadership. Taking 'creativity' first, this has been defined as 'the process of bringing something new into being'. Creativity requires 'passion and commitment' and brings 'to our awareness what was previously hidden and points to new life'.[6] The notion of using creativity in social advancement is central to John Paul Lederach's idea of the moral imagination, mentioned in Chapter Three. Art and culture – and the creativity that underlies them – are vital ingredients of change in a complex non-linear world where the logical framework is only good for the technocratic aspects of development. They can help us replace a materialist account of the universe with one in which we are in touch with higher elements of ourselves.

A critical question is how to bring creativity into the public domain. Research by Fisher and Williams suggests that there are four main conditions that foster creativity in learning situations: motivation, inspiration, gestation and collaboration. The last of these overlaps with the analysis of how networks bring progressive change and therefore has special importance.[7] Creative collaborations can occur spontaneously but leadership is required if they are to survive and to sustain changes in the world. Indeed, leadership is an essential quality if creativity is to be adapted into a means of social advance.

Such leadership needs to be appropriate for the situation. A top-down, command-and-control style of leadership, which may be appropriate in the military or in mass production manufacturing, is not appropriate for managing creativity in networks. A different model of power is needed. In top-down leadership, relations are transactional, whereas in collaborative situations, relationships are participative. It is this latter type of leadership that is most apt in most situations requiring social advance – because power is shared. The architect of this approach is Mary Parker Follett, an early 20th-century feminist writer on management. Writing in the 1920s, she explained that 'power is not a pre-existing thing which can be handed out to someone, or wrenched from someone'. Coining the term 'transformational leadership', she stressed the importance of 'power with' as opposed to 'power over' in producing positive change.[8] A 'power with' model sees power as a self-developing capacity rather than a fixed asset or possession that can be divided, shared, transferred or conferred. This means that power is something developed between people rather than the possession of an individual. In this model, power is constantly reconstructed in the relationships between people. Such a sharing perspective overrides much of the damage done in social development by what 13th-century poet Rumi called the 'thieves of the heart' – greed, ego, anger and insecurity.

Building a constituency

Through holding events, both public and private, to discuss the emerging findings from its work, the Webb Memorial Trust has aimed to build a constituency for that work. People who received grants have been invited to take part in shaping the agenda for the Trust. A key vehicle for discussions has been the All Party Parliamentary Group on Poverty. This has allowed a range of conflicting views to be discussed with the goal of taking the best ideas forward regardless of their political provenance.

In pursuing the work, it would be useful to conduct what Kurt Lewin called a 'forcefield analysis' in which stakeholders of change are analysed according to their relationship with any desired change.[9] This divides people and organisations into four categories: those who will make the change, those who will encourage it, those who will let it happen, and those who will stop it. A key feature of this approach is to get beyond stereotypes and look for 'counterintuitive allies' in the change process. This entails remaining open about who fits into which category and thinking about how to shift people into a more positive role.

This was in evidence during a Trust workshop with community activists and volunteers in Hull, where two small groups addressed this issue. One group worked on an 'asset-based approach to development with groups that aren't like us'. Among the new groups they wanted to contact was business, but not with a view to asking them what companies could give. Rather, they wanted to show them what community groups could contribute, effectively saying to them: 'we have access to communities that you want'. Another group wanted to challenge 'fear' because it is a huge factor and surfaced in so many ways during the meeting – fear of different communities, fear of different ideas, fear of losing what we have. Overcoming fear is a necessary step in breaking out of familiar routines and methods of communication. Their suggested method was to invite some 'unlikely allies' to the next meeting. 'Maybe we will change their mind', said one, 'or maybe they'll change ours.'

Relationship building lies at the heart of building a constituency. This takes time, patience, and personal and social skills. It was striking that during various Hull workshops there was little mention of money: what matters in building a constituency is listening to people, respecting them, investing in them, acknowledging their aspirations and helping provide the means for them to be realised. A meeting of Hull community activists and students held in March 2017 resented the fact that "people and places like Hull are too often defined by a deficit – what they lack – rather than an asset, what they have". People want, as one person put it at the meeting, "trustworthy and accountable institutions. Erosion of faith in some public services is replaced with community solidarity". Practical solutions include: "Make people more aware of their rights and power and replicate this activity with young people to build empathy." Central to the thinking is using 'power with' as an extensible resource which grows with use.

The central purpose of the network is to create energy within a supportive ecosystem that delivers social advance. It is clear from the Trust's work that if we want to make change, it is important to harness the energies of people who want to do things, not to support those who are merely trying to put things back the way they used to be. The sections that follow set out to identify the sources of energy that will deliver the society we want. This may involve entirely new approaches or revivifying old ones in ways that suit the future and not the past. To explore the possibilities, the Trust commissioned studies on various groups in society, looking specifically at what groups do now and what they might do in the future to use their comparative advantage to build a good society without poverty. The Trust commissioned studies on the role of business, planners, voluntary and community sector, fairness commissions and community activists.

The work is far from comprehensive. There are undoubtedly many important people and initiatives out there that are pursuing new forms of action that can contribute to taking forward the principles behind the society we want. What follows is designed to illustrate possibilities. Most of the groups covered are facing a tough time with low capacity, yet there are signs of energy that could be harnessed so that people from different spheres of life could come together to build the society we want.

Business

The Trust commissioned Slack Communications to investigate the role of business in addressing poverty. This entailed a programme of interviews and meetings, together with roundtables hosted by the All Party Parliamentary Group on Poverty.

Why business doesn't see 'poverty' as its business

The starting point for the discussion was that poverty is everyone's problem, and everyone has a role to play in creating a society where we can all thrive. When discussion turns towards the contribution business can make to alleviating poverty, the conversation often falters, or stops altogether.[10] Business leaders argue that poverty is not an issue that is core to their corporate objectives; that it is the responsibility of government or charities; and that any poverty reduction measures would involve high costs and further red tape to negotiate. Even if a company is willing to act, it usually takes the form of a donation to a relevant charity rather than changes to its operations.

As John Mills, economist and founder of consumer goods company JML, stated during a roundtable to discuss the role of business in reducing poverty: 'Most businesses see themselves only to a fairly limited extent as having a role in this issue. Especially around pay, most businesses do not see it as their role to pay more than the market expects.'[11] At a meeting of the All Party Parliamentary Group on Poverty, Peter Kenway reported on in-depth interviews with 20 employers in Scotland who are paying the living wage. He suggested that while they are comfortable discussing poverty as something 'out there' in the community, to be dealt with through Corporate Social Responsibility (CSR) activities such as mentoring in schools, they aren't comfortable with the idea of links between poverty and their core business activity.

Making the economic case

Kenway found that if you want to talk to employers about poverty, it's better to use different language, with terms like fairness and staff wellbeing. Employers talk about fairness, but this is not just altruism: they also talk about the wider value to their business. For very small employers starting out, deciding to pay the living wage differentiates them from the low-wage sector and shows they are exercising leadership. It creates a positive image with employees and customers. The living wage is understood and approved of by the public; it is a standard that businesses can sign up to and thereby improve their image. An employer in a remote community will hope that paying the living wage will encourage the workforce to stay. So this is about self-interest with a wider remit – not just cost minimisation.[12]

This encapsulates the main finding from the research undertaken by Slack Communications. To make progress with businesses, it is important to shift the conversation away from businesses addressing poverty because it is a worthy thing to do, and instead to talk about the commercial advantages it might entail.

Moreover, Slack Communications found a strong economic case for business to tackle poverty. Research has shown how poverty, and the associated physical, mental and emotional impacts, contributes to reduced productivity and loss of income for businesses. A study by Barclays Wealth and YouGov, for example, found that one in ten people employed in the UK are struggling to make ends meet and using expensive forms of borrowing. Some 20 per cent of respondents felt that their financial troubles affect their productivity at work. Overall, the study found that financial stress hurts bottom lines by about 4 per cent a year. Elsewhere, a report by the University of Cambridge found that sickness caused by stress, anxiety or depression cost the economy around £23.8 billion in 2010. In today's straitened times, few sensible businesses are actively looking to increase their costs. However, evidence from the Living Wage Foundation suggests that paying the living wage enhances the quality of staff and improves recruitment, retention and absenteeism. Coupled with increased productivity, this adds up to a considerable return on investment.

It isn't only about higher pay

Slack Communications also found that the response from business to employee hardship doesn't have to involve higher pay alone. Employers can also provide financial and debt advice and counselling, all aimed at helping their workers to manage their resources more effectively. These lower-cost interventions can help people greatly. One in five of the workers surveyed by Barclays felt they would benefit from such services.

Other options are to offer cheaper travel or childcare vouchers or flexible working that enables staff to fit in work around caring responsibilities. At an All Party Parliamentary Group on Poverty meeting, Clare Ludlow of the Timewise Foundation cited a study which found that 46 per cent of the UK workforce wants to work flexibly. This includes people otherwise left out of the labour market – parents, people with disabilities, people returning to work after a gap, and older people. Only 6 per cent of job advertisements paying more than £20,000 full-time equivalent offer flexible or part-time working options, which makes it very hard for a mother or father needing to balance work and children.[13]

Rainy day savings schemes are another option. This echoes a suggestion made by Kevin Hollinrake MP, also at an All Party Parliamentary Group on Poverty meeting, that employers should be more supportive of employees at difficult times. This involves seeing employees as individuals rather than as a group, and identifying what help they need.

There are also advantages to businesses taking steps to tackle poverty within the wider community. Attitudes towards the role of business within society are shifting, and an increasing number of people – particularly millennials – have high expectations that a business will do good as well as make money. From food to fashion, the political and moral viewpoints of many modern consumers have a direct influence on their buying decisions, alongside price and quality. Ethical consumerism is a growing market, worth £32.2 billion and up by 9 per cent between 2012 and 2013, according to the Ethical Consumer

Markets Report from the Co-operative Group. The report also found that roughly 20 per cent of the UK population boycotts specific products or outlets, for a variety of reasons including perceptions around labour standards and tax avoidance. Again, the response to this does not need to be expensive, just creative. A bank could provide free financial advice to people on low incomes; a clothes shop might offer a discounted suit for someone who can prove they have a job interview; a food retailer could work with local businesses to offer discount vouchers for their staff.

Focusing on productivity and employee wellbeing

So how can we change the narrative around the role of business in helping to create a good society that is free from poverty? How can we ensure that the private sector both understands and is willing to play its part? Slack Communications suggests that we need a new conversation, one that focuses on measures that improve productivity and employee wellbeing at the centre. One that recognises that 'business' is not just one homogeneous group but an eclectic mix of micro, small, medium and large companies, all with their very different needs and challenges.

And one that keeps it simple. Those who contributed to the research suggested that societal challenges shouldn't be presented as insurmountable while the solutions should be easy and cost-effective to understand and implement. Increases in red tape should be avoided. Importantly, business should be celebrated not denigrated, as sometimes occurs with poverty campaigners. Overall, we need to highlight that by working together with other societal actors, business can be both financially successful and a powerful force for good.

New models of business

New models of business fit for the 21st century are also beginning to emerge. *Big Issue* founder John Bird stresses the role of social business, with all profits going back into the business rather than to shareholders. His dream: the complete transformation of business so we have social

Amazons and social Tescos. 'We can't leave it to the big guys', he says. 'Consumer power could create a new form of business, social business, providing the same services.'[14] An emerging business model gaining traction around the world is 'B Corp'. Certified B Corporations look after all stakeholder interests and not just those of the shareholders. They voluntarily meet high standards of transparency, accountability and performance.

Planners

Why planning has become marginal

Planning and planners are in the doldrums. In a report commissioned by the Trust in 2013, the Town and Country Planning Association (TCPA) reported that planning is marginal and has little relevance to distributional outcomes for people most in need:

> The reason for this failure is partly because planning is no longer recognised as a mainstream part of public policy in poverty reduction, and because national planning policy has de-prioritised social justice as an outcome.[15]

This, despite a comment in the same report: 'Planning has played a "transformational" role in improving the quality of life in all our communities.'

History shows that the development of planning was associated with the major advances that took place in the middle decades of the last century. The roots of the planning movement go way back to the 19th century, finding expression in Sir Ebenezer Howard's idea of the 'garden city' and his forming of the Town and Country Planning Association in 1899. In *New Jerusalems*, Evan Durbin's daughter Elizabeth charted the historical evolution of planning in the Labour Party.[16] But it was during the war that the idea found favour as all three major parties planned the peace. Planning was a key instrument in 'Butskellism' (a joining together of the names of the Conservative politician R.A. Butler and the Labour politician Hugh Gaitskell). In land use planning, the key instrument was the Town and Country Planning Act 1947, which was a triumph for those who wished to see an orderly and well-regulated environment. By 1949, Evan Durbin famously declared: 'We are all planners now.'[17]

As seen in Chapter One, the 'enterprise culture' of the 1980s swept away restrictions and regulations because it was felt that 'red tape' inhibited economic growth. In land use planning, the Localism Act 2011 is the culmination of 30 years of this approach. It focuses on: 'cutting central targets on councils, easing the burden of inspection, and reducing red tape ... breaking down the barriers that stop councils, local charities, social enterprises and voluntary groups getting things done for themselves.'[18]

A positive role for planning

Such an approach, the TCPA believes, places too much emphasis on economic development and too little on social justice.[19] To revivify planning, the organisation developed #Planning4People. This is a coalition of organisations and individuals who share a common belief in the value of place making to achieve a just and sustainable future. The objective is 'to bring about the rebirth of the creative social town planning which did so much to lay the foundation of a civilized Britain'. The guiding principles are that planning should be democratic and fair, with people at the heart of the process; guided by a powerful definition of sustainable development which emphasises social justice as a key outcome; powerful, so it can regulate change; and responsible so that it meets the basic needs of those who struggle most today, without restricting the ability of future generations to live decent lives.[20]

The goals of the #Planning4People manifesto are very close to the principles for a good society without poverty articulated in Chapter Three. The TCPA is highly active in promoting the idea and more than 100 key people and institutions are registered supporters. It has engaged with hard-to-reach groups to mainstream the ideals of planning through innovative methods such as performing at the Hay

Festival and commissioning a short film of interviews with a range of people talking about why planning is important to their everyday lives.

These are encouraging beginnings. The TCPA is building an entirely new relationship with a wide range of stakeholders, encouraging them to cascade support and information through their constituencies. There is more to be done, but the principle behind their work is that unless we come up with an inclusive plan for our society, we will continue to drift into the society we don't want.

Voluntary and community sector

What potential has voluntary and community action for developing a good society and dealing with poverty? In 2014, the Trust published a supplement in the *New Statesman* under the title: *Taking action on poverty: Does civil society hold the answer?*[21] A range of authors showed that austerity has meant tough times for many organisations, with redundancies, reduced budgets, or even closure. There are opportunities too. There is now widespread agreement that the state must rely more on what people do for themselves, and this offers a way for voluntary organisations to reconfigure themselves to play a significant role in creating an active society, rather than playing second fiddle to the state.

The main study in this area was led by Paul Bunyan and John Diamond of Edge Hill University.[22] They found that civil society has no coherent strategy to tackle poverty, in part because too much emphasis is placed on charitable giving and too little on the causes of poverty. While continuing to remain at arm's length from party politics, voluntary organisations could usefully develop the power of grassroots organisations to engage with, and contest, state and market practices that diminish human dignity. This would entail a more radical approach in favour of the most marginalised in our society.

This was borne out by follow-up work commissioned from Katy Goldstraw and John Diamond. They ran 20 workshops with 'third sector' voluntary and community organisations in England, Scotland, Northern Ireland and Wales. They found some examples of excellent work by the voluntary sector. For example, they studied the role of the voluntary sector in relation to food security:

> Examining poverty alleviation through the lens of food aid reveals a complex and multi-faceted picture of civil society at its best: of volunteering, positive action encapsulated in everything from garages, churches, delivery vans and buildings; of civil society, action organised by independent organisations, small community groups and national voluntary and community sector franchises.[23]

They concluded that people in the voluntary sector are well-meaning and thoughtful about their values, and knowledgeable about what needs to be done in diverse spheres such as economic development, poverty, arts and education. However, they have no overall conceptual frame for their work, which leads to a dissipation of the effort involved. There is a cacophony of voices, which means that there is no coherent message and an overarching tendency to see the government as 'rescuer' for our society and the ultimate focus of their work. While many speak of the importance of 'speaking truth to power', there are few signs of voluntary organisations gaining much leverage with local or other authorities over and above what is entailed by their role in delivering public services, or of meaningful connections with grassroots groups that would give more legitimacy to their concerns. People from voluntary organisations were aware of these concerns. The Belfast group suggested the following challenges:

> '[We] need to protect civic space, to create a cohesive social justice narrative. [We] need a broader engagement from the public – to help understand what they want it to be for. [We] need a model of leadership based on service framed in love.'

Writing in *Third Sector* about the crisis in the charitable sector, leading commentator Joe Saxton has pointed out that 'there is little sign that charities are pulling together for the common good'.[24] But the voluntary sector could be a considerable force for change, and there is much goodwill and much potential there. If charities and voluntary bodies were to unite around common values and a set of focused principles, we would see a joined-up voice of the voluntary sector that would become much more effective than at present. It is a question of leadership.

Fairness commissions

The research also looked at 'fairness commissions'. The first such body was set up in Islington in 2010 and was co-chaired by Professor Richard Wilkinson, co-author of *The spirit level: Why equality is better for everyone*. This book, an international bestseller, generated much debate, positing that societies with a big gap between rich and poor are bad for everyone in them, including the well-off. The idea took off and fairness commissions spread to other places.[25]

Fairness commissions take different forms and have different relationships with their local authority; some are close to them and others entirely independent. Most follow a parliamentary select committee model, enquiry based, taking evidence and producing a final report. Evidence and information is gathered in many ways, including public meetings, listening exercises, themed 'select committee' style meetings, walkabouts, street surveys, web-based surveys and expert presentations to name but a few. Public participation has been central to the process.

Many of the reports highlight stark inequalities. For example, the Tower Hamlets report *Time to act* says that 'there is arguably nowhere in the country where inequality is more pronounced', contrasting the shiny towers of Canary Wharf and the billions generated there to the 49 per cent of children in the borough who live in poverty, the highest proportion in the country. In the Sheffield report inequalities in life expectancy are expressed by reference to the 65-minute journey on the number 83 bus route: at its start at Millhouses in Ecclesall ward, female life expectancy is 86.3 years, but 40 minutes into the journey in the Burngreave ward female life expectancy drops to 76.9 years. [26]

Katy Goldstraw and John Diamond included fairness commissions in their research.[27] The work was based on interviews with 13 fairness commissions, two roundtable discussions and a survey. Findings are based on what fairness commissions say about themselves. Generally, people interviewed felt that fairness commissions have been an effective and useful framework to address local issues and to tackle the issue of fairness within local authorities in a strategic and collaborative way. At their core is a listening approach and as a result the understanding of their areas' needs has increased. People interviewed felt that the fairness commissions have been involved in a meaningful listening exercise.

Councillor Andy Hull, one of the co-chairs of the Islington Fairness Commission, highlighted the following benefits for the council in undertaking the fairness commission:

- The fairness commission provided Islington Council with clarity and simplicity of definition – people know what the Council is about and what it stands for.
- The commission put flesh on the bones of the 'fairness in tough times' mantra.
- It provided a rationale for the tough decisions the Council has to make.
- The commission enabled the Council to exercise influence outside of its authority.[28]

At the same time, it is difficult to identify positive changes in inequality. While evaluation and capturing the impact was built into the work of some commissions, others did not have the budget to fund this. The result was that some commissions wrote their report and then lacked the funding to manage the implementation. Moreover, fairness commissions have no legal or statutory power to address poverty and inequality. They have raised awareness of the issues and attempted to persuade and influence. Goldstraw and Diamond question whether fairness commissions should be more explicit about what they can achieve (raising awareness) and what they cannot (removing poverty and inequality). The main value of fairness commissions has so far been in injecting energy into the debate about inequality rather than finding solutions for the issue.

Community action

This section looks at the question of local people doing things for themselves. While mutual aid was the bedrock of working class society until the 1940s, it went into steep decline after that. In the last of his trilogy on the welfare state, William Beveridge urged the new apparatus of the welfare state to capitalise on people's capacity for mutual aid, but he was ignored.[29] Continued decline has meant that we now live in a more selfish society in which people tend to care less about those outside their friends and immediate family circle, particularly if they are poorer or in some way different from themselves. The culture of citizenship has been weakened by the top-down nature of the institutions of the welfare state, where people are classed as clients, and by the materialist culture of capitalism, where people are classed as consumers.[30] The infrastructure supporting community development has declined, with support organisations such as Community Matters and the Community Development Foundation going out of business in recent years.

However, there are signs of change and increasing calls for community development to be revived. In Hull, for example, there is a growing band of community activists looking for the #hullwewant. Given that neither the economy nor the public sector can deliver the kind of society that Hull people want, a group of local people and organisations have come together to build a network of mutual aid using shared resources. This tackles one of the characteristic weaknesses of the voluntary and community sector, which is its tendency to pursue narrow organisational interests competing for resources and so failing to build a powerful local civil society. The Hull activists see that a powerful local civil society involves fostering cooperation and mutuality to build a culture of sharing between people and collective use of resources.

The activists realise that their ability to do things in traditional ways has been depleted in recent years. Given that many voluntary projects have disappeared and the local authority has half the money it had six years ago, they need to find different ways of doing things, 'looking for a fresh perspective beyond fire-fighting and funding bids'. A key question is 'how can we use what we have to get what we need?' A local community worker explained how they plan to do this:

'The method is mutual aid. Using Timebank, in which people give an hour and get an hour, and Hull Coin, which enables people to trade good deeds for discounts in local stores, we harness the power of local people. This makes the vision a reality where money is the last option rather than the first. This stops things getting stuck when we have a lack of money!'

Community activists organised a 'feastival' in Hull. This was a collective action around food organised within a few weeks. It was designed to be fun and based on generosity. It wasn't owned by any one organisation but built on a sense of trust that already existed. There was no individual or organisational ego involved, and anyone could take part. The experience of collective organising feeds back into that sense of trust and increases it. A virtuous circle is created. As one of those involved pointed out, 'It's not a box-ticking exercise. Everyone can have this and everyone can contribute.'

The group now has 63 youth work and community development students on placements across the city of Hull based on a joint venture to produce the #hullwewant. Taking forward the agenda does not depend on a fixed plan: it draws on resources that already exist to take the 'I' and make it 'we'. The plan is to work across communities with an emphasis on people – not people as funders or representing organisations or political parties, but people who might cooperate with each other based on feelings of solidarity. The community activists in Hull have decided that resources won't stop them from creating the #hullwewant. A meeting of 25 activists devised seven principles to guide their actions:

1. 'We have what we need already. Grow it. Grow networks in Hull for the society we want.'
2. 'Find hidden allies and target gatekeepers.'
3. 'New "pinking". We will change the world.'
4. 'Spark conversations that cascade a vision of Hull people want.'
5. 'Reimagining better futures with young people.'
6. 'Seek a different approach to create positive change and new opportunities.'
7. 'Choose someone to have a conversation with who you wouldn't normally talk to.'

In the final group session, groups were invited to pick one element of a new narrative they would work on, one thing they would do together, and one resource they needed to do it. Here is their answer:

'We have what we need. Let's harvest what we have.'

This chapter has shown the importance of answering the question 'who does what to develop a good society without poverty?' and given some preliminary answers. The question left hanging in the air at the end of this chapter is 'how do we organise it?' This is the topic of the next chapter.

Notes

[1] Orton, M. (2016) 'Creating a shared vision', Webb Memorial Trust Supplement, *New Statesman*, 21 October, p 5.

[2] Orton, M. (2016) 'Whose responsibility is poverty?' Speech at All Party Parliamentary Group on Poverty Event on 26 October 2016, pp 4–5, available from www.appgpoverty.org.uk/wp-content/uploads/2016/10/WebbNSeventlaunch-transcriptfordistribution.docx.pdf

[3] Mason, P. (2015) *Postcapitalism: A guide to our future*, London: Allen Lane, p 263.

[4] Toynbee, A.J. (1961) *A Study of History* (in 12 vols), Oxford: Oxford University Press.

[5] Coleridge, S.T., Engell, J. and Bate, W.J. (1984) *Biographia literaria, or, Biographical sketches of my literary life and opinions* (Vol 7), Princeton, NJ: Princeton University Press.

[6] See the resources on creativity at: www.creativityatwork.com/2014/02/17/what-is-creativity

[7] Fisher, R. and Williams, M. (2004) *Unlocking creativity: Teaching across the curriculum*, London: Routledge.

[8] Follett, M.P. (1995) 'Power', in Graham, P. (ed) *Mary Parker Follett: Prophet of management: A celebration of writings from the 1920s*, Washington, DC: Beard Books, pp 97–120.

[9] Lewin K. (1951) *Field theory in social science*, New York: Harper and Row.

[10] Collinge, T. (2016) 'Why addressing poverty is good for business', Webb Memorial Trust Supplement, *New Statesman*, 21 October.

[11] Mills, J. (2015) Contribution to All Party Parliamentary Group on Poverty breakfast meeting to discuss Webb Memorial Trust research on 'business and poverty', House of Commons 4 March.

[12] Kenway spoke at an All Party Parliamentary Group on Poverty meeting on 3 May 2016. This was written up by Hartnell, C. (2016) 'What is the role of business in reducing poverty in the UK?', available from www.webbmemorialtrust.org.uk/latest-news/blog-what-is-the-role-of-business-in-reducing-poverty-in-the-uk/

[13] Claire Ludlow's contribution to the meeting along with that of Hollinrake is given by Hartnell, C. (2016) 'What is the role of business in reducing poverty in the UK?', available from www.webbmemorialtrust.org.uk/latest-news/blog-what-is-the-role-of-business-in-reducing-poverty-in-the-uk/

[14] John Bird said this at an All Party Parliamentary Group on Poverty meeting on 3 May 2016. This was written up by Hartnell, C. (2016) 'What is the role of business in reducing poverty in the UK?', available from www.webbmemorialtrust.org.uk/latest-news/blog-what-is-the-role-of-business-in-reducing-poverty-in-the-uk/. The Ethical Consumer Markets Report for 2016 is at www.ethicalconsumer.org/researchhub/ukethicalmarket.aspx. This shows a rapidly growing market valued at £38bn in 2016.

[15] Ellis, H. and Henderson, K. (2013) *Planning out poverty: The reinvention of town planning*, London: TCPA and Webb Memorial Trust, p 4.

[16] Durbin, E. (1985) *New Jerusalems: Labour Party and the economics of democratic socialism*, London: Routledge and Kegan Paul.

[17] Durbin, E.F.M. (1949) *Problems of economic planning*, London: Routledge and Kegan Paul.

[18] Communities and Local Government (2011) 'A plain English guide to the Localism Act', November, Department of Communities and Local

Government, p 1, available from: www.gov.uk/government/uploads/system/uploads/attachment_data/file/5959/1896534.pdf

[19] Ellis, H. and Henderson, K. (2014) *Rebuilding Britain: Planning for a better future*, Bristol: Policy Press.

[20] The #Planning4People Manifesto has been developed by the Town and Country Planning Association and is available at: https://www.tcpa.org.uk/planning4people

[21] Webb Memorial Trust (2014) 'Civil society and poverty', Webb Memorial Trust Supplement, *New Statesman*, 2 May.

[22] Bunyan, P. and Diamond, J. (2014) *Civil society and its role in reducing poverty and inequality in the UK*, Ormskirk: Edge Hill University and Webb Memorial Trust.

[23] Goldstraw, K. (2015) 'A literature review: the response of civil society to poverty and inequality in the UK in recent decades', Conducted by Edge Hill University on behalf of the Webb Memorial Trust, p 36, available from: www.edgehill.ac.uk/i4p/files/2014/09/March-2016-Poverty-The-Good-Society-Civil-Society-and-Food-Aid-I4P-Webb-report.pdf

[24] Saxton, J. (2017) 'The sector badly need its own Cobra', *Third Sector*, 30 January.

[25] Wilkinson, R. and Pickett, K. (2010) *The spirit level: Why equality is better for everyone*, London: Penguin Books.

[26] Fairness Commission Tower Hamlets (2013) 'Time to act', November, p 3, available from www.towerhamlets.gov.uk/Documents/One-TH/Fairness-Commission-booklet.pdf. Sheffield Fairness Commission (2013) 'Making Sheffield fairer', January, p 13, available from: www.sheffield.gov.uk/content/dam/sheffield/docs/your-city-council/our-plans,-policies-and-performance/Fairness%20Commission%20Report.pdf

[27] Goldstraw, K. and Diamond, J. (2016) 'A good society: A collaborative conversation', Edge Hill: Edge Hill University and Webb Memorial Trust, available from: https://www.edgehill.ac.uk/i4p/i4p-webb-memorial-trust/

[28] Bunyan, P. and Diamond, J. (2014) *Approaches to reducing poverty and inequality in the UK: A study of civil society initiatives and fairness commissions*, a report commissioned by the Webb Memorial Trust and the All Party Parliamentary Group on Poverty. Available from: www.webbmemorialtrust.org.uk/uncategorized/civil-society-and-poverty

[29] Beveridge, W.H. (2014) *Voluntary action (works of William H. Beveridge): A report on methods of social advance* (Vol 3), London: Routledge.

[30] Knight, B. (2012) 'From big society to good society', *New Statesman*, 23 October.

SIX

Towards transformation

A key message of this book is the need to rethink the problem of poverty. The welfare state narrative that informed social policy in the 30 years following the Beveridge Report has lost its power, and needs to be replaced if we are to make progress. 'Poverty' cannot be the starting point because the word divides people emotionally and politically, so that policies to address poverty always have limited support.

Where we have got to so far

This book has developed an alternative formulation based on building 'the society we want'. The advantage of this approach is that it frames the task positively. Rather than solving a problem that many people feel is of doubtful importance, the goal is to develop an asset that everyone has a stake in. The process should be creative, and avoid the destructive feelings that surround the word 'poverty'.

Notwithstanding the complexity of the issue, five principles have been developed that express what many people want from their society:

1. We all have a decent basic standard of living.
2. So we are secure and free to choose how to lead our lives.
3. Developing our potential and flourishing materially and emotionally.

4. Participating, contributing and treating all with care and respect.
5. And building a fair and sustainable future for the next generations.

In developing these principles, 'the tyranny of perfection' has been put to one side. The principles are a 'good enough' starting point to address the gap between the society we have and the society we want. There is an impressive consistency in what people want – security, fairness and independence – with an emphasis on social values rather than economic ones.

The term 'security' is important as the first building block of a good society. It is also a better entry into social policy than 'poverty', because it is positively framed, has resonance across society, and finds favour among all political parties. This makes it easier to build agreements, which is essential if society is to make the social advances needed to heal the divisions exposed by Brexit.

It is one thing to produce a narrative; quite another to use it to bring about social advance. Society has been drifting for more than 30 years, guided only by the mantra of 'growth and more growth'. During that period, social policies have not worked well and there is nothing immediately on offer to dig us out of the hole that we are in. The thousands of reports published each year by universities, think tanks and charities typically make recommendations to government as rescuer, when it is not at all clear that government wants to act to reduce poverty further or has the capacity to add more policies to its existing commitments.

If we continue to hide behind rational appeals to government, we will not make the advances that we need. The answer lies with people, ordinary citizens and their organisations. Rather than looking to the supply side of governance, we need to look to the demand side and develop people-led action. Only by developing society organically from within, not by seeking technocratic policy fixes, can we develop the society we want. A good society is found as much in the process as in the product, so we need to do this for ourselves. This entails using a new model of power, one that is more inclusive and ensures that the agents of social progress include a wider set of actors than at present. It is particularly important to involve people who are affected by poverty. This entails disturbing the power pyramid to develop a society that everyone feels part of, while reframing the role of the market and public authorities.

The question arises: how to develop a new approach in such a way that it can take root? A blueprint and recommendations would not work: that approach would be a top-down one, a replication of the practice that has become so inimical to social progress. What can be done is to develop a framework based on the research findings that may enable people to think about creative ways to reform society. As a starting point, a clear, broad-based agenda for the society we want must be developed. The next section expands on this and subsequent sections consider pathways for achieving it.

The society we might have

What kind of society would we have if we were to get what we want? It is hard to imagine this when our conventional behaviour is based on tinkering with this or that policy to adjust the system at the margins, rather than looking at the whole thing and envisioning what we might want. As noted in Chapter Three, we are rusty when it comes to thinking about the big normative questions around how to live. We tend to think within a frame of narrow realism and base everything on immediate practicalities, rather than use our moral imagination to design our world afresh.

In addressing the big picture, it is helpful to draw on 'Economic possibilities for our grandchildren' – the article by John Maynard Keynes referred to in Chapter Four.[1] Writing amid the economic turmoil of 1930, Keynes looked ahead to the world of 2030. He suggested – despite the 1929 economic crash – that our long-term economic prospects were bright. He predicted that a combination of growth in wealth and developments in technology would free us from the tedium of work within 100 years.

Such advances would produce a state of 'economic bliss'. This would enable us to 'occupy the leisure, which science and compound interest will have won' and to 'live wisely and agreeably and well'. We would be free from the need to concern ourselves with economics, and able to 'prefer the good to the useful'. Our greatest problem would be to rid ourselves of the work ethic and find constructive ways to use our leisure.

Keynes was remarkably prescient. We have made enormous economic advances and are now on the threshold of an age where technology could largely banish work from our lives. We have sufficient resources for people to be economically secure and socially free to pursue leisure in ways of their choosing. Rather than seeing automation as a threat that will take our jobs, it gives us the option to remove the drudgery of tedious jobs from our lives. Keynes quotes the traditional epitaph of the charwoman:

> Don't mourn for me, friends, don't weep for me never,
> For I'm going to do nothing for ever and ever.

Keynes' imagined world of 2030 gives insight into how we might realise the five principles identified as central to a good society, while becoming both 'secure' and 'free'. Economic bliss brings security and the resulting leisure brings freedom. Such a scenario could be the salvation of humanity. As individuals, we could use leisure to develop our creativity, engage in lifelong learning and, if so inclined, enhance our spirituality. As social beings, we could spend more time with our families and friends. As active members of society, we could contribute through voluntary work and concentrate on making our planet beautiful and sustainable, developing a new respect for nature while reaching out to people from different cultures to improve the cohesion of our societies. Our world would resemble the Buen Vivir movement in Latin America, which is based on the principles of harmony between human beings and nature, as described in Chapter Four. In short, we could create the social bliss to accompany the economic bliss. In so doing, we would banish the fear and hatred that stem from our insecurities.

Organising for a good society

Having set out a narrative for a good society, the next step is to organise it. As soon as we begin to think about this, we encounter a major stumbling block. This is Keynes' mistaken assumption that, once a certain level of wealth had been achieved, people would feel that they had enough so that making money would play second fiddle. Keynes predicted that in 2030:

> The love of money as a possession – as distinguished from the love of money as a means to the enjoyments and realities of life – will be recognised for what it is, a somewhat disgusting morbidity, one of those semi-criminal, semi-pathological propensities which one hands over with a shudder to the specialists in mental disease.

Far from taking second place, money continues to be an obsession with the rich. In 2010, according to Oxfam International, the wealthiest 388 people on the planet possessed as much wealth as the poorest half of the world's population. By 2012 this figure was 159, in 2014 it was 80, and in 2015 it was just 62.[2] Luna Glucksberg and Roger Burrows have recently reviewed the literature on how the very rich create infrastructures to ensure the reproduction of dynastic wealth.[3]

While so much of the earth's wealth belongs to so few people, it is hard to see how the rest can be secure and free. With such wealth comes enormous power, and rich people show few signs of wanting to change anything. Although new wealth has produced new foundations, they typically address charity rather than justice.[4] If we want to see a fairer world, civil society organisations will need to play a key role. This entails shifting the power so that it comes from below not above.

Chapters Two and Five showed the strength of thousands of people and organisations working for a better world; but also the weakness of efforts that are splintered, divided and competitive. There is no social movement that joins together efforts to improve the environment, reduce poverty, raise the status of women, guarantee human rights for oppressed groups such as migrants and refugees, and combat racism. Civil society lacks a coordinated strategy so that there is a cacophony of voices. While some see infighting as a democratic virtue,[5] significant advance has been made only when good leaders with an explicit change agenda organise a mass of people. Chapter Four traced the link from John Ruskin through to Gandhi, Martin Luther King and Citizens UK. There is a thread of change-based literature running through the work of Paulo Freire,[6] who saw education as a process in which people can transform the world about them, to Saul Alinsky in his community-organising manual *Rules for radicals*,[7] and Anne Firth Murray, whose *Paradigm found* has become the basis of women's empowerment across the world.[8] These books demonstrate that real progress can be made when people organise for change with a noble aim, use a responsible method, and ensure that they serve both the self-interest of the participants and the wider public interest. Effective approaches entail replacing standard methods based on hierarchy and competition with feminist principles of respect, reciprocity, cooperation and inclusivity. The work of the Global Fund for Community Foundations to #ShiftThePower in international development is an example of how this can be done.

A critical step is to develop the narrative about the society we want. Setting out five principles for a good society without poverty is a first step. A 2014 YouGov survey suggests that this would be popular. The survey suggests an 'inequality moment' has been reached since 56 per cent would like to see a more equal distribution of wealth even if it reduces the total amount of wealth, while only 17 per cent would choose greater overall wealth even if it leads to greater inequality.[9] The Trust research supports this view, a common observation being, as one focus group participant put it, "While there is such a divide in wealth, I don't think we can ever have a good society." "It's all down to resources and wrong distribution that creates the imbalance in the world", said another. This has consequences for who has opportunities. "It's wrong that we don't all start from a level playing field", said one. "We need equality of opportunity", said another, while a third said, "It's absurd that some people have so much, while so many have so little".

Having said that, the research also suggests that the word 'inequality' is not a good basis for organising. There is a widespread perception that activists who promote equality are 'left-wing' and their language, as one focus group member put it, "smacks of communism". In contrast, the idea of 'security' works well. "What we need", said another focus group member, is "security for all."

Security first

'Security for all' offers a starting point. It has the potential to rally disparate interests in the way that Citizens UK did when it developed the idea of the 'living wage'. If civil society organisations could think and act collaboratively, share assets between organisations and think about long-term systemic change in favour of 'security for all', they could not only develop a new way of seeing but also ensure that other sectors took it seriously.

To investigate the idea of a joint approach to security, the Trust sponsored eight workshops between November and December 2016 in various parts of the UK. They were organised and led by Michael Orton. A total of 145 people attended. Around a third of participants were frontline advice workers. Another third were from third sector organisations including charities, campaign groups, housing associations, think tanks and organisations such as credit unions. There were some local authority workers and academics. Some had direct experience of poverty.

The workshops came up with many suggestions for the future of the social security benefits system but there was no consensus. The debates within groups were often fruitless. Interviews with 12 leading social security experts confirmed that there is no consensus on social security and no forum to develop agreement on ways forward. This is clearly an area that requires further attention.

One promising area for further work is the idea of a basic citizens' income. This is a simple idea, growing in popularity, to pay an unconditional monthly allowance to cover basic needs such as food, shelter and education to every individual as a right of citizenship.[10]

Rutger Bregman's research claims that the approach works because it removes the sense of scarcity that leads to the failure of anti-poverty programmes.[11] This finding is supported by Mullainathan and Shafir, whose research demonstrates that people on low incomes are so preoccupied with meeting their basic needs that they have insufficient 'bandwidth' to take advantage of educational or training programmes designed to help them get out of poverty.[12] In a recent *Guardian* article, Bregman notes:

> When it comes to poverty, we should stop pretending to know better than poor people. The great thing about money is that people can use it to buy things they need instead of things self-appointed experts think they need. Imagine how many brilliant would-be entrepreneurs, scientists and writers are now withering away in scarcity. Imagine how much energy and talent we would unleash if we got rid of poverty once and for all.[13]

However, financial modelling shows that it is hard to design a revenue-neutral basic income scheme that pays a decent sum without creating significant numbers of losers among people on means-tested benefits. This is because the current benefits system, with its reliance on means testing, can pay relatively large sums to groups with complex needs. A flat-rate scheme cannot compensate for the withdrawal of both personal tax allowances and most means-tested benefits without becoming expensive.[14]

At the same time, all the evidence suggests that radical reform of the benefits system will become necessary and desirable as it become clearer that well-paid work will no longer support the mass of the people. In his bestselling book *Homo deus*, Yuval Noah Harari predicts that the 'data universe' driven by algorithms will produce a world where labour is redundant and society is divided between the 'super rich' and the 'useless class'.[15] Without economic or military purpose, new fictions will be needed to make sense of the world. This dystopian vision is the converse of Keynes' economic bliss.

Avoiding such a world would mean national government taking on the role of guaranteeing people's basic needs to enable citizens to take responsibility for moving to a higher platform in their lives. Such a perspective is found in Beatrice Webb's Minority Report, in which the job of the state is 'to secure a national minimum of civilised life open to all alike, of both sexes and all classes', by which she meant 'sufficient nourishment and training when young, a living wage when able-bodied, treatment when sick, and modest but secure livelihood when disabled or aged'.[16] So long as there is the sense that the system is for everyone, the method of achieving this is less important than the principle of doing so. While any method would be expensive, costs could be set against the £78 billion estimated to be spent on compensating for poverty each year.

People power

While the state guarantees the basics, Beatrice Webb's view was that voluntary action should provide services 'that are placed firmly on the foundation of an enforced minimum standard of life and carry out the work of public authorities to finer shades of physical and moral and spiritual perfection'.[17] This 'extension ladder model' involves a sharp distinction between state and voluntary action. The state does the basics; voluntary action the rest.

The research found many examples of local voluntary action playing an important role. In 2014, following the sad and unexpected death of a popular member of parliament, the Trust supported the All Party Parliamentary Group on Poverty to administer the Paul Goggins Memorial Prize. This sought nominations from members of parliament for the best voluntary project in their constituency with evidence to show that it was reducing poverty. The 34 entries contained a high proportion of foodbanks. What was interesting was that the projects did many other things as well as addressing food poverty. The winner was the Whitefoot and Downham Community Food Project. In accepting the prize, Councillor Janet Daby noted that food is important, though she also stressed:

'the story is of a community building relationships and being mutually supportive. We need each other, to offer support and to help one another. Building strong communities is needed, whether it is to listen, to socialise, to give advice, support with decision making, finding employment, support with child care and so on. We also need to reduce the isolation and fear that many people really do experience. As people, we are stronger when we do things together.'

This is an example of local grassroots action that is taking place up and down the country. Small in scale and often operating below the radar, such efforts rely heavily on local people as volunteers. Such behaviour is found in every community; it is a naturally occurring asset often overlooked by large funders seeking large-scale impact. Being small is a virtue because it allows intimacy, and the value of such work is in the social and community cohesion that it produces.

Recognising and supporting such work is vital if we are to address the sense of disconnection people feel from their societies which found expression in the Brexit result. Small-scale local action can transform culture away from the money-making ethos to one based on the five principles set out in this book. Association and participation of ordinary people are not only the underlying processes that make communities work but also the means through which our understanding of values is transmitted in our society. Such processes of association and participation were the building blocks of the great transformative movements of the 20th century, including civil rights and feminism. In planning the future, it is vital that we harness the energy of people in their relationships. It is clear from the research that there is much energy for a more participative society and that, given the opportunity, people want to move forward. What follows is a selection from 42 statements about what they intend to do next made by Hull University students at a workshop to develop the #hullwewant:

- 'Find people's strengths to facilitate their learning journey, create a positive cycle.'
- 'Bring communities together to work with what they have and what they want for the future.'
- 'Raise critical consciousness in young people about their rights.'
- 'Develop a collective project across communities to stimulate communication and build the foundations of Hull together rather than in individual areas.'

An ecosystem of local relationships

This sort of local action needs to take place within the context of a supportive framework of relationships with other organisations. As Amy-Grace Whillans-Wheldrake, winner of the New Statesman/Webb Memorial Trust 2016 essay prize, put it:

> The debate around community resilience must therefore move beyond placing sole responsibility on communities to develop a holistic approach ... This will require the commitment and development of long-term relationships between key stakeholders, services and communities, alongside significant time and resource commitments.[18]

This implies that progress depends on an ecosystem of supportive relationships. The Trust commissioned work on this from Neil McInroy, who drew on extensive research by the Centre for Local Economic Strategies.[19] The following sections owe much to his work and are designed to give tools to people who want to develop a good local society.

McInroy began by asking: 'Can we begin to recouple the fundamental link between the social and economic drivers within our economic systems and harness them to reduce poverty and create a more equal and just society?' The answer is yes, he says, and is best expressed in local places with local identities. It is here that the intimate relationships and reciprocity between citizens, state and businesses can be remade. It is also where families live and where poverty is experienced.

The current push for the devolution of powers and resources to local government and cities represents an opportunity to link economic, public service and anti-poverty goals.[20] The devolution of powers and resources to local government and cities could facilitate a greater democratisation of the economy and create an important forum for addressing poverty. Indeed, argues McInroy, freed from the constraints of central government, the development of forms of economic activity that fit more securely with local characteristics and social needs could bring a significant anti-poverty dividend. First, we need to address our values.

McInroy suggests that, to build a good local society, we need a 'local economy that develops empathy'. He uses the work of Enlightenment thinker Adam Smith. While Smith is best known for propagating the idea of self-interest in economic exchange, he also considered the wider moral motivations and institutions required to support economic activity in general.[21] Smith recognised that sympathy, ethical considerations and societal norms and values play an important role as motivations for an individual's economic activity. Smith tells us we have two vital interdependent elements in society: benevolent self-interest and a need to empathise with the social plight of others.

However, the world of economic policy continues to overplay 'self-interest', seeing the economic sphere as a distinct and opposite pole to the social sphere. The two spheres are and should be one and the same. The aim of the economy should be to improve social conditions. Wealth creation should not just be about private gain; it is primarily about the development of human and social life and a decent standard of living for all.[22] For Smith, the purpose of an economy is to 'generate the necessary commodities for the support of life whatever the custom of a country renders it indecent for people even of the lowest order to be without'.[23] The aim of an economy must therefore be to enable people to live the lives that they want. Markets must serve to generate both social and economic freedoms and opportunities to operate effectively. If an economy fails to create these opportunities, it can be said to be unjust.[24]

On this model, tackling poverty and inequality becomes an intrinsic and fundamental part of achieving local prosperity and reforming public services. Instead of local communities being viewed as mere downstream recipients of economic success (as beneficiaries of actions designed to deliver agglomeration and 'trickle-down' growth), they are active upstream parts of a system that creates success in the first place. The example given in Chapter Five of how local people are organising in Hull shows how this could work. On this model, social development and tackling poverty (in the form of more jobs, decent wages, rising living standards and civic pride) should be seen less as a mere consequence of economic development action and more as something that is interwoven with it. Economic efficiency is an important goal, but so too is social equity and fairness. This entails authorities delegating as much power to local action as possible using the 'principle of subsidiarity'. The *Oxford English Dictionary* defines subsidiarity as 'the principle that a central authority should have a subsidiary function, performing only those tasks which cannot be performed at a more local level'.

The question again arises of 'how to make this happen'. Again, following the logic of the research findings, a blueprint for this cannot be set out, but some suggestions can be made about processes that may yield benefits. McInroy suggests following the work of Roberto Unger, who stresses the importance of social innovation.[25] The approach entails thinking and working across all sectors – public, private and community – in new ways. The essence is to experiment and use small-scale innovations to foreshadow the possibilities of larger-scale transformations in society.

McInroy gives many examples of this approach. This book will give two: cooperative councils and local currency. Plymouth has a philosophy of working on cooperative principles according to which the council empowers residents to take greater control of their own lives. As part of this, the '1,000 Club' is an alliance between senior public sector leaders and businesses to help young people become ready for work. Some 580 businesses are involved and 1,639 opportunities for young people have been created. Other local authorities are copying the model. In Brixton, there is an experiment with local currency. The Brixton Pound is about 'money that sticks to Brixton'; the currency is used among local traders and is exchangeable for sterling at a ratio of 1:1. The idea is that money spent with independent businesses circulates within the local economy up to three times longer than when it's spent with national chains. The approach has been followed in other places, including Totnes, Bristol, Lewes, Stroud and Hull.

Young people need to be part of these processes. They are particularly valuable when it comes to seeing solutions to old problems. They are adept with technology and need to be inducted into positions of power if they are to help to undo some of the messes created by their elders. In most efforts to involve young people, their participation is tokenistic. Greater openness in thinking is needed if we are to turn this around. This point will be returned to later in the chapter.

A framework for local development

While social innovation and youth involvement are important, on their own they do not provide a framework for developing policy and practice beyond being on the lookout for good ideas and finding ways to bring them to scale. The Centre for Local Economic Strategies has developed an agenda for local development, which may be helpful. The essence of the approach is set out under seven headings as follows:

1. Place

A sense of place is central. The local authority has a key role because, notwithstanding austerity, it is the owner of land and buildings and has considerable purchasing power. It can act as convenor across different institutions and networks, and enable an atmosphere of self-determination and creativity among local people and community groups.

2. Collaboration

Local authorities can foster the development of a fully cooperative council in which many actors are involved. The emphasis is on developing businesses owned by local people and creating an environment in which local people have power in their communities.

3. Anchor institutions

Organisations that have an important presence in a place (for example, hospitals and universities and other large employers) can be involved in sustainable economic practices, buying goods and services locally and ensuring local people are fairly treated in hiring policies.

4. Business

Business is not seen as part of the problem but as a full partner in the development of place. This involves a shift from business policies based on 'corporate social responsibility' to 'corporate citizenship'. This follows the kind of approach set out in Chapter Five.

5. Citizens

There are strong links between social capital and economic prosperity that are important in tackling poverty. Local people and their networks are important as co-producers through being partners in a sharing economy. This stresses the value of solidarity and is overlooked in much current thinking about the economy.

6. Work

Employment support is best designed and delivered at local level. Local employers have a key role in developing a living wage and ensuring that people have access to training.

7. Wealth and supply chains

Procurement policies need to ensure that, as far as possible, wealth created locally remains in the local economy.

McInroy has developed a table to show the changes under each of the headings that need to take place to realise this agenda (Table 6.1).

Table 6.1: Changes that need to take place to realise a local agenda for development

Agenda item	Traditional approach	Good local society approach
Place	Top-down, centralised governance	Devolution of decision making based on systems thinking
Collaboration	Decisions made by elites (business and local governments)	Plurality of decision making based on cooperation
Anchor institutions	Isolated	Part of connected ecosphere
Business	Wealth creators and corporate social responsibility	Business as citizens
Citizens	Recipients of policy	Participants in policy
Work	Scant regard for wages or conditions	Decent jobs and place-based employment charters
Wealth and supply chains	Based on efficiency and trickle down	Based on community wealth and local social value

Source: Table 6.1 has been reproduced from McInroy, N. (2016) *Forging a good local society: Tackling poverty through a local economic reset*, Centre for Local Economic Strategies and Webb Memorial Trust. The original is 'Figure 4. Summary of agendas for a good local society in contrast to traditional approaches' on page 24

This is a radical approach. It requires a rethinking of the relationships between local communities, local authorities and central government. Making it work involves double devolution. While central government gives new powers and responsibilities to local government, including the ability to fund itself, local government gives power and control to local people.

A critical piece is citizen engagement. In Osborne and Gaebler's view, community members can add special knowledge, motivations and experience that professionals and bureaucrats cannot possess.[26] They quote John McKnight of Northwestern University, who suggests that communities are better able to understand and address their problems than government professionals because they are closer to them. Public agencies can nurture community control by encouraging communities to take control of services; by providing seed money, training and technical assistance; and by removing bureaucratic hurdles. An interesting model to examine would be experiments to offer 'new careers for the poor', which were one of the most successful ventures in the American 'War on Poverty' during the 1960s.[27] While letting go of the reins, government is still ultimately responsible for ensuring services reach those who need them, that structures are in place to identify corruption, and that decentralised programmes are working properly.

The role of national government

So far, this book has stressed the importance of the local dimensions in addressing poverty and developing the society we want. This is an important corrective to the prevailing discourse which sees national government as the principal agent responsible for policy on poverty and related matters.

We need both local and national. Part of the national role would be to have an overarching plan about what kind of society we want. Such a plan would have two main goals: first, to ensure security for all citizens; second, to empower citizens to develop the society that they want. This is based on Sidney and Beatrice Webb's extension ladder model of government in which the state provides the basics and people do the rest. As suggested earlier, this will involve building a society based on 'having enough' rather than 'everlasting growth'. This policy framework would ensure that resources are used in favour of the five principles set out in this book and that social factors are given as much weight as economic ones. Resource allocation, taxation and regulation would be developed on that basis.

National government would also act directly on issues that can only be driven nationally. The main priority would be guaranteeing the economic and social security of citizens. Again, policy directions cannot be prescribed, though ideas have emerged from the research for *Secure and free*.[28] The issue of social security benefits was considered earlier in this chapter. This is important because a key part of security is having enough to live on. Another important issue is having somewhere to live. We saw in Chapter Two that housing has a big effect on poverty rates for some groups.

Housing

The Trust commissioned Birmingham University to examine the policies that would underpin the role of social housing in a good society. Their report suggested that policy makers should look to the principles that drove early postwar public housing. This entails a flexible mix of tenures, with councils and housing associations providing both social and private rented homes. This 'hybrid' approach would 'help restore civil society roles in housing and allow a greater emphasis on community stewardship'.[29]

The report was used to stimulate discussion among 15 housing experts, academics and people in the voluntary sector, who were asked to write short blogs reflecting on housing policy.[30] Several important themes emerged from this exercise. First and foremost, central government has a key role to play in increasing the supply of housing. At least 250,000 new homes each year are required, but the private sector has never produced more than 150,000 homes and it is not in their interests to build more. Private sector construction must therefore be supplemented with a combination of council, housing association and community-led housing.

Since increasing the supply of social housing will not fully solve housing poverty, other measures are important. Given that poverty is now closely associated with private renting, where overcrowding, cold, damp and high energy costs are common problems, there is a strong case for the registration of private sector landlords, together with annual inspections and greater powers of intervention for local authorities. Security for tenants could be improved through a 'right to sell' and 'right to stay', so that those who can no longer afford mortgage repayments can sell their properties and remain as tenants paying fair rents.

One problem is that different housing markets make universal solutions difficult. Brian Robson from the Joseph Rowntree Foundation suggests that Scotland, Wales and Northern Ireland have put in place policies that are successfully meeting their housing needs, while England is making little or no progress.

Although not as extreme as with social security, the issue of consensus also emerged here. According to Kate Henderson,[31] chief executive of the Town and Country Planning Association, we must build a consensus that housing – including housing that is available for social rent, from either a council or a housing association – is good for the nation. Advocates need to explain why new housing is both necessary and desirable as a pillar of a civilised society. This will require reform of the planning system since some of its outcomes are plainly against the long-term public interest. If we want to ensure a legacy of beauty and durability for our children and grandchildren which truly meets the challenges of the 21st century, we urgently need to restore a comprehensive framework of place-making standards, and to rebalance planning policy so that social justice outcomes are given as much weight as the needs of landowners and developers. Much can be learned from the garden cities, as found at Letchworth and Welwyn, which represent the very best of British place making and a successful financial model based upon the capture of the uplift in land values which the granting of planning permission and the development creates. This can be used to fund infrastructure provision, debt repayments and long-term reinvestment in the new community.

Towards the next generation

The task of this book has not been to provide answers but to provide a fresh framework through which others can develop answers. It has also been mindful of the future. Transformation relies heavily on the people responsible for it, and the Trust's work with children and young people suggests that the coming generation is more likely to make change than the current one. Powerful ideas are coming from young people. They can find consensus because they do not have the baggage of older generations and are not hemmed in with institutional categories that diminish creative thought.

Today, baby boomers run our country. Because of their sheer demographic power, they have fashioned the world around them in a way that meets all their housing, healthcare and financial needs. David Willetts shows how the baby boomer generation has attained this position at the expense of their children.[32] He argues that if our political, economic and cultural leaders do not address the future, the young people of today will be taxed more, work longer hours for less money, have lower social mobility, and live in a degraded environment to pay for their parents' quality of life. Evidence suggests that the older generation tends to base its attitudes on nostalgia, which is why it was overrepresented in the recent referendum among those who wished to put the clock back to the time before Britain was a member of the European Union.[33]

The research findings suggest that it is time for a new generation of young people to lead the way. Rys Farthing and Sara Bryson,[34] who led the work with children from low-income parts of England, have shown that very young people can produce ideas that will take us beyond the failed narrative on poverty and usher in a good society. They see themselves as having the capacity to make choices, and able to make the 'right' decisions to improve their finances when they need to. Far from the accusations of laziness and apathy, these young people are incredibly ambitious and optimistic about their own capacities.

In a recent article, Rys Farthing has demonstrated the multitude of ways in which today's young people are actively trying to improve their chances.[35] First, younger generations appear *en masse* to be taking the individual gamble of investing in their education – they are the most educated generation ever despite the personal debt they are incurring. Second, they seem to be trying new forms of collective action, such as occupying and hacking, that sit outside the two-party political regime and which few boomers seem willing to recognise as legitimate. Other groups of young people are actively organising to reduce poverty in more traditional ways. For example, a group in the North East that took part in action research commissioned by the Trust is running a campaign to end holiday hunger.

It's time to listen to and work with young people to support them in achieving the future that they want. All the evidence suggests that they understand what needs to be done to replace the failures of their elders with a world that offers both security and freedom. What we need is not a set of transactional policies that shift resources, but the development of transformational relationships that shift power.

Notes

[1] Keynes, J.M. (2010) 'Economic possibilities for our grandchildren', in *Essays in persuasion*, Palgrave Macmillan UK (pp 321–32). Available from: www.econ.yale.edu/smith/econ116a/keynes1.pdf

[2] Oxfam International (2016) 'An economy for the 1%: How privilege and power in the economy drive extreme inequality and how this can be stopped'. Available from: www.oxfam.org/en/research/economy-1

[3] Glucksberg, L. and Burrows, R. (2016) 'Family offices and the contemporary infrastructures of dynastic wealth', *Sociologica*, 10(2), pp 1–23.

[4] McGoey, L. (2015) *No such thing as a free gift*, London: Verso; Knight, B., Mahomed, H. and Sahai, C. (2013) 'Good sibling; bad sibling: Philanthropy and inequality', *Alliance*, 18(2), June.

[5] Greta, C. (2017) 'Six reasons why the left should keep on infighting', *Transformation*, 17 March. Available from: www.opendemocracy.net/transformation/greta-christina/six-reasons-why-left-should-keep-on-infighting

[6] Freire, P. (1970) *Pedagogy of the oppressed*, Harmondsworth: Penguin Books.

[7] Alinsky, S. (2010) *Rules for radicals: A pragmatic primer for realistic radicals*, New York: Vintage.

[8] Murray, A.F. (2011) *Paradigm found: Leading and managing for positive change*, Novato: New World Library.

[9] The YouGov study is available at: https://yougov.co.uk/news/2014/04/30/equality-more-important-wealth

[10] Torry, M. (2013) *Money for everyone: Why we need a citizen's income*, Bristol: Policy Press.

[11] Bregman, R. (2017) *Utopia for realists: How we can build the ideal world*, London: Hachette UK.

[12] Mullainathan, S. and Shafir, E. (2014) *Scarcity: The true cost of not having enough*, London: Penguin Books.

[13] Bregman, R. (2017) 'Utopian thinking: The easy way to eradicate poverty', *The Guardian*, 6 March.

[14] Reed, H. and Lansley, S. (2016) *Universal basic income: An idea whose time has come?*, London: Compass.

[15] Harari, Y.N. (2016) *Homo deus: A brief history of tomorrow*, New York: Random House.

[16] Webb, B. (1948) *Our Partnership*, London: Longmans, Green & Co, pp 481–2.

[17] Webb, S. and Webb, B. (1912) *The prevention of destitution*, London: Longmans, Green and Company. p 252.

[18] Whillans-Wheldrake, A. (2017) 'In the light of Brexit, what can low income communities in the UK do to organise themselves to become more resilient and self-sufficient?', *New Statesman*, 6 January 2017, p 32.

[19] McInroy, N. (2016) *Forging a good local society: Tackling poverty through a local economic reset*, Manchester: CLES and Webb Memorial Trust.

[20] Information about the devolution agenda can be found at: http://researchbriefings.parliament.uk/ResearchBriefing/Summary/SN07029

[21] Sen, A. (2010) 'Adam Smith and the contemporary world', *Erasmus Journal of Philosophy and Economics*, 3(1), pp 50–67.

[22] Roberts, R. (2015) *How Adam Smith can change your life: An unexpected guide to human nature and happiness*, London: Portfolio Trade.

[23] Smith, A. (1979) *The wealth of nations*, Harmondsworth Penguin, first published in 1776, pp 889–90.

[24] Eiffe, F. (2008) *The Smithian account in Amartya Sen's economic theory*, Institute for Social Policy, Department of Economics University Vienna.

[25] Unger, R. (2007) *The self awakened: Pragmatism unbound*, Cambridge, MA: Harvard University Press.

[26] Osborne, D. and Gaebler, T (1992) *Reinventing government: How the entrepreneurial spirit is transforming the public sector*, Boston: Addison-Wesley.

27 Pearl, A. and Riessman, F. (1965) *New careers for the poor: The nonprofessional in human service*, New York: Free Press.

28 Orton, M. (2016) *Secure and free: 5+ solutions to socio-economic insecurity*, London: Compass.

29 Gregory, J., Mullins, D., Redman, P. and Murie, A. (2016) *Social housing and the good society*, Birmingham University, Housing and Communities Research Group. Available from: www.birmingham.ac.uk/Documents/college-social-sciences/social-policy/SPSW/Housing/2017/WMT-final-NOV-12th-Clean-Version.pdf

30 Available at: www.webbmemorialtrust.org.uk/wp-content/uploads/2017/02/Housing-poverty-and-the-good-society-ebook-2017.pdf

31 Henderson, K. (2017) 'Creating successful new communities', in Hacker, P. (ed) *Housing, poverty and the good society: what can we achieve by 2025?* Newcastle upon Tyne: Webb Memorial Trust, available from www.webbmemorialtrust.org.uk/home-page/housing-poverty-and-the-good-society-what-can-we-achieve-by-2025/

32 Willetts, D. (2011) *Pinch: How the baby boomers took their children's future and why they should give it back*, London: Atlantic Books.

33 *Financial Times* data on the demographics that drove Brexit. Available from: www.ft.com/content/1ce1a720-ce94-3c32-a689-8d2356388a1f

34 Farthing, R. and Bryson, S. (2015) 'Poverty ends now', unpublished final report to the Webb Memorial Trust on a Children's antipoverty manifesto based on the work of 38 children from five of the poorest wards in England.

35 Farthing, R. (2016) 'Views from the "selfish" generation', Webb Memorial Trust Supplement, *New Statesman*, 21 October.

Index

grassroots groups 84–6, 147–9
growth 32–3
  'inclusive' approaches 100
  limits of 35, 92–4, 98–100

H

happiness studies 91
Harford, Ian 42
Harris, John 30
hate crimes 41–2, 62
health impacts of poverty 47
Henderson, Kate 157
Hobbes, Thomas 61
home ownership 31
Homo deus (Harari) 146
household debt 33, 124
household incomes, by different
  groups 44–5
housing 156–7
  costs and poverty 33, 42–5
  land use and planning 48–9,
    127–9, 156–7
  post-war boom 97
  standards for 157
  state-sponsored building
    programmes 108, 156–7
  views on 76–7
housing benefit 100
Hull community workshops
  121–3, 133–5, 148–9
Human Development Index 12

I

IMF 33, 48
immigration 70
  see also migrants
income
  by different groups 44–5
  weekly earnings 23
  see also pay
inequality
  causes of 33

language of 6
pay disparities 33–4
post-2008 crisis 29–30, 33–4,
  99, 143
post-war history 18–21
reaching a tipping point 144–5
risks of 33–4
insecurity and social malaise
  29–30, 124
Institute for New Economic
  Thinking 92–3
intergenerational poverty 46–7
intergenerational wealth 143
Islamophobia 62
Islington Fairness Commission
  131–2

J

Jacques, Martin 39
Jenkins, Simon 32
job security 34
  see also security
Joseph Rowntree Foundation 7,
  8, 37, 40, 42, 47, 95, 157
Judt, Tony 55–6
Just deserts (Coates) 99

K

Kellner, Peter 31
Kenway, Peter 100, 123–4
Keynes, John Maynard 17–19,
  20–1, 93, 141–2, 143
Kickstarter 41
Kincaid, James 18
Krugman, Paul 18
Kuznets, Simon 98–9

L

Labour governments (1997-
  2007; 2007-10) 22–3
labour protection 34
Lagarde, Christine 33

Unger, Robert 151
United States 20, 62
universal credit 23
university access 31
Unwin, Julia 13

V

Varoufakis, Yanis 49
voluntary sector
  as agents for societal change
    129–31, 147–9
  decline of 40–1
  need for 'joined up' practices
    130–1, 143–4
von Hayek, Frederick 2, 19

W

Waldfogel, Jane 22
Washington Consensus 39–40,
  48
Watson, Justin 6
wealth 65–7, 143
  predistribution of 99
Webb Memorial Trust
  on the building of a
    constituency 121–7
  on economic development
    98–100
  on the language of poverty
    5–7
  on myths about poverty 13–16
  on responsibility for poverty
    reduction 117
  research on the making of a
    'good society' 1–4, 63–87
  survey findings and analysis 63,
    64–72, 116–18
  use of participatory research
    72–87
Webb, Beatrice 1–2, 8, 16–17,
  147
welfare benefits

history 17–19, 36, 103
impact of withdrawal 94–5
media representations 20
original purpose 100
perceived importance of 65–7
percentage spent on
  unemployed 14
potential future of 145–7
problems of 103–4
public views on 11, 14, 15–16,
  103–4
Webb's 'extension ladder
  model' 147, 155
welfare reform 23, 94–5
'Welfare to Work' programmes
  95
Westen, Drew 15
Whillans-Wheldrake, Amy-
  Grace 149
Wilkinson, Richard 48
Willetts, David 158
women's empowerment 144
working families, in poverty
  42–5, 95, 99
working tax credits 22, 100

Y

YouGov survey 63, 64–9, 90–1,
  117, 144–5
  analysis 69–72
young people
  job insecurity 34
  leading societal change 158–9

Z

zero-hours contracts 33–4